The ASCA National Model: A Framework for School Counseling Programs

AMERICAN
SCHOOL
COUNSELOR
ASSOCIATION

Citation Guide

When citing from this publication, use the following reference:

American School Counselor Association (2003). *The ASCA National Model: A Framework for School Counseling Programs.* Alexandria, VA: Author.

1101 King St., Suite 625, Alexandria, VA 22314
(703) 683-ASCA, (800) 306-4722, fax: (703) 683-1619
www.schoolcounselor.org

ISBN 1-929289-02-2

Table of Contents

V. Management System

VI. Accountability System

VII. Implementation

VIII. Appendix

Foreword

Standardizing the practices of an entire profession is an enormous undertaking, but for school counseling, it is necessary. The profession has suffered from a lack of consistent identity, lack of basic philosophy and, consequently, a lack of legitimization. ASCA wishes to thank Judy Bowers and Trish Hatch, Ph.D., who took on the task of developing The ASCA National Model: A Framework for School Counseling Programs, which was above and beyond their responsibilities as ASCA Governing Board members. The work of developing the model is their gift to ASCA and to school counselors across the country. They researched history, collected and analyzed state documents, conducted conversations, synthesized material and wrote the program handbook. Their joint efforts have produced a document intended to guide a state, district or school through the process of designing, developing, implementing and evaluating a school counseling program committed to enhancing high achievement for every student.

Judy Bowers, Ed.D.

"Thank you to Tina Ammon, Ed.D., for providing the leadership and vision for the state of Arizona in the late 1980s and early 1990s to develop a comprehensive competency-based guidance (CCBG) program. Thank you to the school counselors in the Tucson Unified School District and to the counselors in Arizona for their dedicated work since 1990 to develop and refine a CCBG program. Their yearly work at the Arizona Counselor Academy has been used as a guide in the development of the ASCA National Model. Thank you to the leadership in the Tucson Unified School District during the last 13 years for allowing me to be involved in state and national initiatives for school counseling programs. I especially appreciate the support provided in allowing me to be involved in creating The ASCA National Model: A Framework for School Counseling Programs."

- Judy Bowers, Ed.D. 2003

Trish Hatch, Ph.D.

"In 1997-98, a task force of Moreno Valley Unified School District (MVUSD) school counselors began transforming the district's program to align with ASCA's National Standards. The following year, all counselors started measuring program results, leading to both state and national awards. A special thank you to these dedicated school counselors who each year create action plans, measure results, lead, advocate and promote systemic change. Many of the forms, samples and examples in this document were taken from the Moreno Valley program and the work of its school counselors. Thank you also to the administration and School Board of MVUSD who supported my efforts in this project and my involvement with professional associations, the California Department of Education for its consultation, the Riverside County Office of Education for its grant and the Riverside County school counselors who piloted the model."

– Trish Hatch, Ph.D., 2003

Acknowledgements

Many school counseling books and materials were used in the preparation of this program model. It is a compilation of theory, practices, documents and writings from the national leaders in the field of school counseling. ASCA would like to extend its sincere appreciation to the authors of the following documents who have graciously contributed their work to the creation of the National Model. Their work has influenced the document, been adapted to varying degrees and infused throughout The ASCA National Model: A Framework for School Counseling Programs.

Arizona Department of Education (2002). *Arizona Counselor Academy program handbook*. Tucson, AZ: Center for Educational Development.

Bowers, J. L. & Colonna, H. A. (2001). *Tucson Unified School District guidance and counseling program handbook*. Tucson, AZ: Tucson Unified School District.

Campbell, C. A. & Dahir, C. A. (1997). *Sharing the vision: The national standards for school counseling programs*. Alexandra, VA: American School Counselor Association Press.

Dahir, C. A., Sheldon, C. B. & Valiga, M.J. (1998). *Vision into action: Implementing the national standards for school counseling programs*. Alexandria, VA: American School Counselor Association Press.

Gysbers, N. C. & Henderson, P. (2000). *Developing and managing your school guidance program*. (3rd Ed). Alexandria, VA: American Counseling Association.

Hatch, T. & Holland, L.A. (2001). *Moreno valley unified district school counselor academy handbook*. Moreno Valley, CA: Moreno Valley Unified School District.

Henderson, P. & Gysbers, C. N. (1998). *Leading and managing your school guidance staff*. Alexandra, VA: American Counseling Association.

Johnson, C. D. & Johnson, S. K. (1997). *Results-based student support programs.* San Juan Capistrano, CA: Professional Update.

Johnson, C. D. & Johnson, S. K. (2001). *Results-based student support programs: Leadership academy workbook.* San Juan Capistrano, CA: Professional Update.

Martin, P. J. & House, R. M. (2002). *Transforming school counseling in the transforming school counseling initiative.* Washington, DC: The Education Trust.

Myrick, R.D. (2003). *Developmental guidance and counseling: A practical approach.* (4th ed). Minneapolis, MN: Education Media Corporation.

The Education Trust (2002). *National school counselor initiative: Met Life Foundation.* Washington, DC: Author.

ASCA wishes to thank the many organizations, school counselors and administrators who previewed ASCA's National Model for School Counseling Programs.

Thank you to Lori Holland, who provided an invaluable service as scribe, organizer and first-line editor; to ASCA's communications director, Kathleen Rakestraw; to Mark Kuranz for his excellent leadership skills as chair of the model committee; and to Peggy Hines and Paul Meyers, who provided detailed feedback and assistance.

ASCA acknowledges and thanks the many state departments of education, school counseling associations and school districts that shared documents to be reviewed in the writing of this book. Their names are listed in the appendix.

Preface

ASCA is indebted to the three professionals who for many years led the counseling profession to new horizons by challenging where the profession had been and suggesting where it might be going. Their participation in the development of the National Model and the ASCA Annual Conference in June 2002 was historically significant. Following are their reflections and their vision for the future of school counseling.

The Center of Education

Norman Gysbers, Ph.D.
University of Missouri-Columbia

My vision for guidance and counseling is for every school district in the United States to have a fully implemented comprehensive guidance and counseling program, serving all students and their parents and staffed by active, involved school counselors working closely with parents, teachers, administrators and community members. When guidance and counseling is organized and implemented as a program, it places school counselors conceptually and structurally in the center of education, making it possible for them to contribute directly and substantially to their local school districts' educational goals. As a result, guidance and counseling becomes an integral and transformative program in the district, not a marginal and supplemental activity.

The program approach not only provides the means and common language across all school district levels for ensuring all students and their parents benefit from guidance and counseling activities and services, but it also provides the foundation for accountability. This approach is results-based, contributing to the achievement of student results, results established by local districts in their school improvement plans. Also, this approach mandates regular review and evaluation of a district's comprehensive guidance and counseling program using program standards; ongoing review and enhancement of the program's content, services and activities; and yearly evaluation of the district's school counselors' performance, using established performance standards.

What is the value-added benefit of having a fully implemented comprehensive school guidance and counseling program in place in local school districts? Research conducted in Missouri (Lapan, Gysbers, & Petroski, 2001; Lapan, Gysbers, & Sun, 1997) has shown that when school counselors have the time, the resources and the structure of a comprehensive school guidance and counseling program in which to work, they can contribute to positive student academic success and student career development as well as to the development of positive and safe learning environments in schools. In Utah, Nelson and Gardner (1998) found that students in schools with more fully implemented guidance programs rated their overall education as better, took more advanced mathematics and sciences courses and had higher scores on every scale of the American College Testing program.

Being involved in developing and implementing a comprehensive school guidance and counseling program may seem overwhelming, but the rewards are substantial. More pride in being a school counselor is evident. More support is generated because guidance and counseling is no longer seen as an ancillary support service. And perhaps most important, students, parents, teachers, administrators and the community are served more effectively. These are the strong messages sent by school counselors and administrators who are using the program approach to guidance and counseling in their school districts.

References

Lapan, R. T., Gysbers, N. C., & Petroski, G. F. (2001). Helping seventh graders be safe and successful: A statewide study of the impact of comprehensive guidance and counseling programs. *Journal of Counseling & Development, 79,* 320-330.

Lapan, R. T., Gysbers, N. C. & Sun, Y. (1997). The impact of more fully implemented guidance programs on the school experiences of high school students: A statewide evaluation study. *Journal of Counseling & Development, 75,* 292-302.

Nelson, D. E., & Gardner, J. L. (1998). *An evaluation of the comprehensive guidance program in Utah public schools.* Salt Lake City: Utah State Office of Education.

We Have Only Just Begun

Sharon K. Johnson, Ed.D
Professor
California State University
Los Angeles

C. D. Johnson, Ph.D.
Counselor Education Professor
School of Psychology
Walden University

We have only just begun the process of discovering and inventing the new organizational forms that will define guidance and counseling programs in the 21st century. We must learn to see the world anew.

Student support programs are at best a series of communities represented in the professional organization that are interdependent and diverse, embracing differences, releasing energy and building cohesion. The broader educational community will be enhanced by the health of the many smaller professions that constitute the whole. Counselors within each community define all community. Building the global community of the future is not the work of tomorrow. We are each called to build it today – to build it now.

The importance of this effort of establishing a guide for school counselors' use cannot be overstated. Through this initial document, ASCA has assumed leadership in beginning the process of discovering and inventing the new organizational forms that will define guidance and counseling contributions in the 21st century. Schools and counseling professionals are called to see the world anew, to build the models and programs of the future and to start today.

The model presented by ASCA is admittedly a composite drawn primarily from three successful models that have many years of research and successful implementation in school districts.

> **66 Whatever is flexible and flowing will tend to grow and whatever is rigid and blocked will atrophy and die. 99**
>
> *from the*
> *Tao of Leadership*

These are the Norm Gysbers and Pat Henderson model, the Sharon Johnson and Curly Johnson model and the Bob Mryick model. The task of the ASCA writing team was a daunting one, to review current, successful results-based models, identify common elements and somehow fit those elements together into a comprehensive model that draws on the best of each selected model. The primary authors of this document, Judy Bowers and Trish Hatch, with the assistance of the executive director, held three meetings that led to consensus on the content by the ASCA Governing Board and other contributors. All agreed that the model presented is only a beginning and guide for the school counselors to use to begin their efforts to establish a comprehensive results-based guidance program that is relevant for their individual school communities. We highly endorse ASCA's model for use as a tool to begin the long process of making the shift to student results-based guidance programs.

A Next Step Into History

Robert Myrick, Ph.D.
University of Florida, Gainsville

It has taken a great number of personal and professional actions to advance school counseling to where it is today. There have been countless events where dedicated counselors consulted with one another and discussed what they were doing in their jobs, what they saw as their mission, what made their contributions unique and what their role should be. The ASCA National Model was created and molded by such counselors through task groups, conferences and committees. It is a significant professional effort and undertaking.

There are thousands of school districts,

and each has a history that reveals how its counseling and guidance program was put in place and evolved. In a school environment, numerous job functions can fall to counselors. Because political and economic conditions often influence the direction and development of student services, the challenges and demands on school counselors can change. The role of a school counselor can and does vary.

History shows that unless the role of a school counselor is clearly established, the whims of the times can threaten the very existence of counselor positions. In addition, many of the early leaders who had a vision for the profession have left their legacy to new generations, many of whom assumed that counselors have always been in schools and that certain tasks and responsibilities have always been in place. In reality, school counseling is a young profession, and like many children growing up, it can flop back and forth while trying to find a clear identity and purpose. Likewise, just as there are parents with different values, needs and home situations influencing children's growth and development, so are there diverse school districts and administrators who have their own ideas of what counselors should do.

We can point to some pockets of excellence, where school counselors have created exemplary programs and implemented successful counselor interventions. We talk about them with pride.

On the other hand, there are school counselors who need help in defining, clarifying and advocating their roles and functions. Some are like a rudderless ship moving with the tides and waves of uncertainty.

The ASCA National Model suggests that school counselors can be more accountable when they follow a universal plan that can be implemented from state to state, district to district and school to school. The model captures the profession's vision of what counselors can do and outlines the fundamental components that characterize an effective and unique guidance program. It can be used to confirm best practices or to spark changes and improvements. It is a bold step that is timely and needed. It is the necessary next step in the profession's distinguished history.

Introduction

School counselors continue to define new directions for their profession as they navigate through the educational landscape of the 21st century. The purpose of ASCA's National Model: A Framework for School Counseling Programs is to create one vision and one voice for school counseling programs. In understanding the school counseling profession's future, it is crucial to understand its past.

At the turn of the 20th century, school counselors did not exist. Instead, teachers used a few minutes of their time to offer vocational guidance to students preparing for work in a democratic society. The school mission of today is not altogether different than in the 1900s. Today, in a world enriched by diversity and technology, school counselors' chief mission is still supporting the academic achievement of all students so they are prepared for the ever-changing world of the 21st century. School counselors do not work in isolation; instead, they are professionals, integral to the total educational program. This evolution from minutes a day to trained professionals implementing a school counseling program is the result of professional scholars, counselor educators, administrators

and school counselors having the vision, knowledge and determination to move forward (Hatch & Bowers, 2002).

School counseling training programs have conflicting and varied theoretical perspectives. Consequently, within the field we have programs that have trained counselors differently. School counselors began as vocational counselors nearly 100 years ago, and the profession has evolved to address all children in the comprehensive domains of academic, career and personal/social development. During this evolution, differing philosophical perspectives developed between and among academic counselors, career counselors, and personal/social or mental health counselors regarding school counselors' role, function, purpose and focus.

In the late 1950s and early 1960s, the National Defense Education Act provided funds to train school counselors. Although some in the field advocated for a directive approach to school counseling, the training school counselors received was heavily influenced by the client-centered view often called the nondirective approach to counseling. Counselors trained in programs rooted in psychological and clinical paradigms differed greatly from those rooted in educational paradigms. These varying perspectives confused and caused role confusion among school counselors, school administrators, teachers, and parents or guardians. In an effort to unify the profession, comprehensive guidance and counseling programs emerged in the 1970s and 1980s (Gysbers & Henderson, 2000; Myrick, 2003).

Historical analyses of earlier program descriptors include "vocational counselor," "guidance counselor" and "guidance and counseling." However, in 1990, ASCA's Governing Board unanimously moved to call the profession "school counseling" and the program a "school counseling program." This change was later reflected in an ASCA statement of the school counselor's role. In 1997, ASCA published "Sharing the Vision: The National Standards for School Counseling Programs" (Campbell & Dahir, 1997) as a conscious effort to participate in the national reform agenda through the development of the ASCA National Standards. This landmark document for the profession, endorsed by national educational and professional organizations, contains student content standards for school counseling programs in the areas of academic, career and personal/social development. "Vision Into Action: Implementing the National Standards for School Counseling Programs" (Dahir, Sheldon & Valiga, 1998) provides school counselors tools for selecting student competencies and suggestions for infusing competencies into the school counseling program. ASCA's National Standards have been widely used in designing content standards for students in school counseling programs.

At its March 2001 meeting, ASCA's Governing Board agreed development of a national school counseling program model was the next logical step to build

on the National Standards. ASCA held a meeting to create a National Model for School Counseling Programs and brought together leaders in the field to create the vision. ASCA moved forward in developing the model to address historical concerns, current challenges within the profession and to assist counselor educators and practicing school counselors in planning for the future of their programs and the profession through one common lens.

The ASCA National Model: A Framework for School Counseling Programs maximizes the full potential of the National Standards documents and directly addresses current education reform efforts. This includes the reauthorization of the Elementary and Secondary Education Act, which emphasizes increased accountability for all federally funded programs.

The ASCA National Model: A Framework for School Counseling Programs is written to reflect a comprehensive approach to program foundation, delivery, management and accountability. The model provides the mechanism with which school counselors and school counseling teams will design, coordinate, implement, manage and evaluate their programs for students' success. It provides a framework for the program components, the school counselor's role in implementation and the underlying philosophies of leadership, advocacy and systemic change. School counselors switch their emphasis from service-centered for some of the students to program-centered for every student. It not only answers the question, "What do school counselors do?" but requires us to respond to the question, "How are students different as a result of what we do?"

ASCA collaborated to develop the model after extensive review and synthesis of state, district and site models,

> **66ASCA has a long and valued history of helping counselors be more effective and efficient in their work.99**
>
> *Bob Myrick, Ph.D., University of Florida*

> ❝This document is not a quick fix but rather a step-by-step pathway to a school counseling program you can be proud of and know you can implement.❞
>
> *Pat Schwallie-Giddis, Ph.D.,*
> *George Washington University*

bringing together the most important current concepts regarding school counseling programs.

Although the model serves as a framework for the development of a school counseling program, it is not meant to be replicated exactly as written here. Effective programs consider local demographic needs and political conditions when integrating and adapting the National Model. The model, therefore, is not intended to be used as a cookie-cutter approach in developing school counseling programs. Rather, ASCA's goal in developing the model is to institutionalize the framework for and process of developing a school counseling program.

In The ASCA National Model: A Framework for School Counseling Programs, the school counselor serves as the program leader. ASCA collaborated with The Education Trust to infuse themes of advocacy, leadership and systemic change throughout the document (*www.edtrust.org*). The program defines the school counselor's leadership role within the school counseling model. The school counselor's leadership skills are important to the successful implementation of new or remodeled programs at the school, district or state level. In this leadership role, school counselors serve as change agents, collaborators and advocates. School counselors must be proficient in retrieving school data, analyzing it to improve student success and using it to ensure educational equity for all students. Through collaboration with other professionals in the school building, school counselors influence systemic change and advocate for students and their counseling program by using strong communication, consultation and leadership skills.

The model incorporates school counseling content standards for every student, focusing the direction for an organized, planned, sequential and flexible school guidance curriculum. The model recommends the use of disaggregated data to drive program and activity development, thus enabling school counselors to intentionally design interventions to meet the needs of all students and to close the gap between specific groups of students and their peers. The model provides an organizational framework and accountability systems to determine how well students have met the standards or have achieved intended outcomes. The school counseling program aligns goals and objectives with the school's mission and ultimately leads to increased student achievement as demonstrated by results data.
The implementation of the ASCA National Model holds great promise for the school counseling profession and the students of this nation. In serving all students equitably, effective school counseling programs become data driven, are annually evaluated and modified based on results. No matter how comfortable the status quo or how difficult or uncomfortable change may be, it is

* In response to concerns regarding whether the National Standards documents are standards for programs or students, the ASCA National Model Task Force concurred at its November 2002 meeting that the ASCA National Standards (Cambell & Dahir, 1997; Dahir, Sheldon & Valiga, 1998) are content standards for student academic, career and personal/social development. The National Standards are for students, not programs.

Other standards are addressed within this document. ASCA program standards (for program audits), ASCA school counselor performance standards (for school counselor evaluation) and ASCA Ethical Standards.

necessary to ensure that every student achieve success. The ASCA National Model promises to direct us away from inconsistent program implementation and expectations toward a united, focused professional school counseling program with one vision in mind.

"We need to be the change we want to see happen. We are the leaders we have been waiting for."

Mahatma Gandhi

A School Counseling Program is...

What is a School Counseling Program?

A school counseling program is comprehensive in scope, preventative in design and developmental in nature. The ASCA National Model: A Framework for School Counseling Programs is written to reflect a comprehensive approach to program foundation, delivery, management and accountability. School counseling programs are designed to ensure that every student receives the program benefits. Historically, many school counselors spent much of their time responding to the needs of a small percentage of their students, typically the high achieving or high risk. The ASCA National Model: A Framework for School Counseling Programs recommends the majority of the school counselor's time be spent in direct service to all students so that *every* student receives maximum benefits from the program.

Comprehensive in Scope

A comprehensive school counseling program will focus on what all students, from pre-kindergarten through 12th grade, should know, understand and be able to do in these three domain areas: academic, career and personal/social. The emphasis is on academic success for every student, not just those students who are motivated, supported and ready to learn. The school counseling program helps all students achieve success in school and develop into contributing members of our society.

Preventive in Design

The purpose of the school counseling program is to impart specific skills and learning opportunities in a proactive, preventive manner, ensuring all students can achieve school success through academic, career and personal/social development experiences. Therefore, the school counselor's duties need to be limited to program delivery and direct counseling services. Prevention education is best accomplished through the implementation of school guidance curriculum in the classroom and through coordination of prevention education programs such as the conflict resolution and anti-violence programs at their sites. The management system section delineates ASCA's recommended use of time for counselors. School counselors can use this guide when planning program services and curriculum including developing a calendar of the year's prevention activities.

Developmental in Nature

School counselors design programs and services to meet the needs of students at various growth and development stages. School counseling programs establish goals, expectations, support systems and experiences for all students. They provide the rationale for school counselors, school administrators, faculty, parents or guardians, businesses and the community to engage in conversations about expectations for students' academic success and the role of counseling programs in enhancing student learning. The student content standards are public statements of what students should know and be able to do as a result of participating in a school counseling program.

> **❝The timing of this model is ideal. Standards-based education has moved the focus of school from entitlement to performance. This has resulted in a shift from teaching to learning in classrooms. For school counseling programs, this means moving from services to programs and from measuring processes to measuring results.❞**
>
> *Paul Meyers, California Department of Education*

The ASCA National Model:
1. establishes the school counseling program as an integral component of the academic mission of your school;
2. ensures equitable access to the school counseling program for all students provided by a state-credentialed school counselor;
3. identifies the knowledge and skills all students might acquire as a result of the K-12 school counseling program; and
4. ensures the school counseling program is comprehensive in design and delivered in a systematic fashion to all students.

Each student content standard is followed by student competencies and a list of indicators enumerating desired student learning outcomes. Student competencies define the specific knowledge, attitudes and skills students should obtain or demonstrate as a result of participating in a school counseling program. These listings are not meant to be all-inclusive, nor is any individual program expected to include all of the competencies in the school counseling program. The competencies offer a foundation for what a standards-based program addresses and delivers. These can be used as a basis to develop measurable indicators of student performance. The standards for academic development guide the school counseling program to implement strategies and activities to support and maximize student learning. Academic development includes acquiring attitudes, knowledge and skills that contribute to effective learning in school and across the life span, employing strategies to achieve success in school and understanding the relationship of academics to the world of work and to life at home and in the community.

The student content standards for career development guide the school counseling program to provide the foundation for the acquisition of skills, attitudes and knowledge enabling students to make a successful transition from school to the world of work and from job to job across the life career span. Career development includes the employment of strategies to achieve future career success and job satisfaction as well as fostering understanding of the relationship between personal qualities, education and training and the world of work.

The standards for personal/social development guide the school counseling program to provide the foundation for personal and social growth as students progress through school and into adulthood. Personal/social development contributes to academic and career success. Personal/social development includes the acquisition of skills, attitudes and knowledge that help students understand and respect self and others, acquire effective interpersonal skills, understand safety and survival skills and develop into contributing members of our society.

Integral Part of the Total Educational Program

The ASCA National Model supports the school's academic mission by promoting and enhancing the learning process for all students through an integration of academic, career and personal/social development. ASCA encourages school counselors to become catalysts for educational change and to assume or accept a leadership role in educational reform. As specialists in child and adolescent development, school counselors coordinate the objectives, strategies and activities of a developmental school counseling program. School counselors are advocates for students as the students strive to meet the challenges and demands of the school system and prepare for transition after high school. School counselors are specially trained educators in a position to call attention to situations within the schools that defeat, frustrate and hinder students'

academic success. School counselors are aware of the data identifying patterns of achievement and behaviors affecting student success. They provide the leadership to assess school needs, to identify issues and to collaborate with others to develop solutions.

The ASCA National Model represents what a school counseling program should contain and serves as an organizational tool to identify and prioritize the elements of a quality school counseling program. It describes the program components and serves as a framework for developing and writing a school counseling program. The ASCA National Model guides states, districts and individual schools in designing, developing, implementing and evaluating a comprehensive, developmental and systematic school counseling program.

Designs a Delivery System

The delivery system (Gysbers & Henderson, 2000) describes activities, lessons and other areas in which counselors work delivering the program. School counselors use the four components below in the systematic delivery of the program.

◆ The curriculum component provides a method by which every student receives school guidance curriculum content in a systematic way.

◆ The individual student planning component provides all students an opportunity to work closely with their parents or guardians to plan, monitor and understand their growth and development and take action on their next steps personally, educationally and occupationally.

◆ The responsive services component responds to the direct, immediate concerns of students and includes, but is not limited to, individual counseling, crisis counseling, referrals or consultations with parents or guardians, teachers or other specialists.

◆ The system support component enables the school counseling process to be effective through: leadership and advocacy, consultation, collaboration and teaming, program management and professional development. This component also provides appropriate support to other programs in the school.

Implemented by a State-Credentialed School Counselor

Professional school counselors are credentialed by their states, and most possess a master's degree. Although teaching experience is not required in some states, it is important for school counselors to receive training in student learning styles, classroom behavior management, curriculum and instruction, student assessment and student achievement.

Conducted in Collaboration

Professional school counselors work collaboratively with parents or guardians, community members and other support services professionals as part of the student support services team. In addition, school resource officers, school nurses, school social workers and school psychologists are all part of the student support system that pulls together, often in the form of a student assistance team, helping students and their families identify student needs and to refer them to appropriate resources both within and outside of the school.

Monitors Student Progress

Monitoring is the process of reviewing data to determine if a student or group of students is demonstrating the desired results as delineated in the program goals and related student competencies. Professional school counselors are expected to consistently monitor and enhance academic progress and achievement. They also advocate for educational and career planning and strive to remove barriers to learning.

Driven by Data

School counseling programs are data-driven. Data create a picture of student needs and provide an accountable way to align the school counseling program with the school's academic mission. Although it is certainly important to know what services are provided for students (process data), this doesn't provide the complete picture. Collecting process data, which is evidence that an event or activity occurred without a clear understanding of the activity's impact (perception and results data), is less meaningful because it does not provide enough information. Results data answer the question, "So what?" Results data show proof that a student competency is not just mastered but has affected course-taking patterns, graduation rates, knowledge attainment, attendance, behavior or academic achievement. In addition, it is important to disaggregate data, which is the process of separating out data by variables such as gender, ethnicity or socio-economic status, to examine equity issues and the needs of various student groups.

Seeks Improvement

The purpose of evaluation is improvement. School counseling programs receive valuable information from measuring results enabling them to determine what is working and what is not. School counselors can use this information to evaluate the program and make necessary adjustments.

Shares Successes

Professional school counselors share their program successes. Informed stakeholders know and promote the value and necessity of school counselors in children's lives. School counselors market and share the results obtained in successful programs with school sites and local, state and national stakeholders who need this information to advocate for the improvement of school-counselor-to-student ratios.

A Cooperative Effort

School counselors collaborate with many stakeholders to ensure a quality school counseling program. Through this cooperative effort, school counseling programs become an integral part of the total school mission.

School counselors manage the school counseling program and ensure effective strategies are employed to meet stated student success and achievement. The school counselor provides proactive leadership, which engages all stakeholders in the delivery of activities and services to help students achieve success in school. School counselors provide direct services to every student.

Teachers work in a partnership role with school counselors, developing and infusing guidance activities into the instructional program. This partnership can be used to extend the attainment of student achievement through collaborative classroom guidance experiences.

Administrators provide support for the organization, development and implementation of the school counseling program. They encourage counselors and teachers to work cooperatively and allow time, facilities and resources to facilitate the process. The administrator recognizes and supports school personnel and community members' important roles in the implementation of the school counseling programs.

Parents or guardians work in partnership with school counselors to help their students be successful in school. They may also serve on advisory or other site committees. Parents or guardians are encouraged to collaborate with school personnel to become involved as advocates for the success of every student.

Students are active participants in the school counseling program and assume responsibility for their success in school. Students and counselors work together to ensure academic success.

Community members such as business, labor and community agencies partner with schools in a variety of ways by volunteering, mentoring and providing sites for student service learning experiences and placements for school-related work programs and field trips.

(Adapted from Arizona Department of Education CCBG Program Model Handbook, 2002.)

> *The National Model for School Counseling Programs will help school counselors become one vision and one voice for students' academic success.*
>
> *Pam Gabbard, Ballard County Elementary School & ASCA President 2001-2002*

Benefits of School Counseling Programs Based on ASCA's National Model

The model provides a system that encourages and promotes academic, career and personal/social development in preparation for the challenges of the 21st century. All stakeholders share the benefits of this organizational structure. School counseling programs have a positive impact on students, parents or guardians, teachers, administrators, boards of education, school counselors, counselor educators, post-secondary institutions and the community. The following benefits have been updated from Sharing the Vision: National Standards for School Counseling Programs (Dahir & Campbell, 1997) to reflect The ASCA National Model: A Framework for School Counseling Programs.

Benefits for Students

- Ensures every student receives the benefit of the school counseling program by designing content curriculum for every student
- Monitors data to facilitate student improvement
- Provides strategies for closing the achievement gap because some students need more
- Promotes a rigorous academic curriculum for every student
- Ensures equitable access to educational opportunities
- Fosters advocacy for students
- Supports development of skills to increase student success

Benefits for Parents or Guardians

- Provides support in advocating for their children's academic, career and personal/social development
- Supports partnerships in their children's learning and career planning
- Ensures academic planning for every student
- Ensures access to school and community resources
- Provides training and informational workshops
- Connects to community- and school-based services
- Provides data for continuous information on student progress
- Ensures every student receives the content of the school counseling curriculum
- Promotes a philosophy that some students need more and seeks to ensure they receive it

Benefits for Teachers

- Promotes an interdisciplinary team approach to address student needs and educational goals
- Increases collaboration with school counselors and teachers
- Supports development of classroom-management skills

- Provides a system for co-facilitation of classroom guidance lessons
- Supports the learning environment
- Promotes teaming to increase student achievement
- Analyzes data to improve school climate and student achievement

Benefits for Administrators

- Aligns the school counseling program with the school's academic mission
- Provides a school counseling program promoting student success
- Monitors data for school improvement
- Provides a system for managing a school counseling program
- Articulates a process for evaluating a school counseling program
- Uses data to jointly develop school counseling goals and school counselor responsibilities
- Provides useful data for grant applications and funding sources
- Provides a proactive school guidance curriculum addressing the students' needs and enhancing school climate

Benefits for the Boards and Departments of Education

- Provides a rationale based on data for implementing a school counseling program
- Ensures equity and access to a quality school counseling program for every student
- Demonstrates the need for appropriate levels of funding
- Articulates appropriate credentials and staffing ratios
- Informs the community about school counseling program success
- Supports standards-based programs
- Provides data about improved student achievement

Benefits for School Counselors

- Defines responsibilities within the context of a school counseling program

- Seeks to eliminate non-school-counseling program activities
- Supports access to every student
- Provides a tool for program management, implementation and accountability
- Recognizes school counselors as leaders, advocates and change agents
- Ensures the school counseling program's contribution to the school's mission

Benefits to Counselor Educators

- Builds collaboration between counselor education programs and schools
- Provides a framework for school counseling programs
- Provides a model for site-based school counseling fieldwork or internships
- Increases data collection for collaborative research on school counseling programs
- Establishes a framework for professional development to benefit practicing school counselors
- Promotes alliances with other educator training programs

Benefits for Post-secondary Education

- Enhances articulation and transition of students to post-secondary institutions

- Prepares every student for advanced educational opportunities
- Motivates every student to seek a wide range of substantial, post-secondary options, including college
- Encourages and supports rigorous academic preparation
- Promotes equity and access to post-secondary education for every student

Benefits for Student Services Personnel

- Defines the school counseling program
- Maximizes collaborative teaming to ensure individual student success
- Uses school counseling program data to maximize benefit to individual student growth
- Increases collaboration for utilizing school and community resources

Benefits for Community: business, labor and industry

- Increases opportunities for business, industry and labor to actively participate in the school counseling program
- Builds collaboration, which enhances a student's post-secondary success
- Connects business, industry and labor to students and families
- Supports the academic preparation necessary for students' success in the workforce

Accountability

Results Reports
School Counselor Performance Standards
The Program Audit

Management System

Agreements
Advisory Council
Use of Data
Action Plans
Use of Time
Calendars

Delivery System

School Guidance Curriculum
Individual Student Planning
Responsive Services
System Support

Foundation

Beliefs and Philosophy
Mission Statement
ASCA Content Standards for Student Academic,
Career and Personal/Social Development

CHAPTER 2

The ASCA National Model for School Counseling Programs

The model graphic, shown opposite, represents the operational structure and components of ASCA's National Model for School Counseling Programs. The graphic contains three levels and four squares, each representing one of the major systems of the model; the arrows in each square point to the systems they influence as in a building-block approach. Note the arrows for the foundation (the first level) lead to the management and delivery systems (the second level). These in turn lead to the accountability system (the third level). Finally, looking closely, one can see how the black arrow points from accountability down to the foundation component. This stresses the importance of using information learned through the accountability process to refine the foundation of an effective school counseling program. The border of the model represents school counselor skills and attitudes of leadership, advocacy and collaboration, which lead to systemic change. These overriding concepts surround and affect the blocks representing the interdependence of the four systems.

Elements of the National Model

Foundation

The foundation provides the *what* of the program, discussing what every student will know and be able to do.

Beliefs and philosophy: The philosophy is a set of principles (usually a set of "we agree" statements) that guides the program development, implementation and evaluation. It is important that all personnel involved in managing and implementing the program achieve consensus on each belief or guiding principal contained in the philosophy.

Mission: A mission statement describes the program's purpose and provides the vision of what is desired for every student. A school counseling program mission statement aligns with and is a subset of the school and district missions.

Domains: The school counseling program facilitates student development in three broad domains, academic, career and personal/social, to promote and enhance the learning process.

ASCA National Standards and competencies: The ASCA National Standards serve as the foundation for the ASCA National Model. Student competencies define the knowledge, attitudes or skills students should obtain or demonstrate as a result of participating in a school counseling program. They are developed and organized into content areas (Campbell & Dahir, 1997).

Delivery System

The delivery system addresses *how* the program will be implemented.

Guidance curriculum: The guidance curriculum component consists of structured developmental lessons designed to assist students in achieving the competencies and is presented systematically through classroom and group activities

K-12. The purpose of the guidance curriculum is to provide all students the knowledge and skills appropriate for their developmental level.

Individual student planning: The individual planning component consists of school counselors coordinating ongoing systemic activities designed to assist the individual student in establishing personal goals and developing future plans.

Responsive services: The responsive services component consists of activities to meet students' immediate needs. These needs may require counseling, consultation, referral, peer mediation or information.

Systems support: The systems support component consists of the professional development; consultation, collaboration and teaming; and program management and operation activities that establish, maintain and enhance the total school counseling program (Gysbers & Henderson, 2000).

Management Systems

The management system addresses the *when* (calendar and action plan), *why* (use of data) and *on what authority* (management agreement and advisory council) the program will be implemented.

Management agreements: School counselor and administrator agreements include statements of responsibilities by each counselor specifying the program results the counselor is accountable for achieving during the year. It also includes how counselors divide the program responsibilities. These agreements are negotiated with and approved by designated administrators at the beginning of each school year.

Advisory council: An advisory council is a group of people appointed to review guidance program results and to make

---

❝The National Model for School Counseling is ASCA's most thoughtful and assertive effort to ensure that school counselors across the nation can provide comprehensive school guidance and counseling programs.❞

Bob Myrick, Ph.D.,
University of Florida

recommendations. The group representatives are student, parents or guardians, teachers, counselors, administration and community members.

Use of data: A school counseling program is data-driven. The use of data to effect change within the school system is integral to ensuring that every student receives the benefits of the school counseling program. School counselors must show that each activity implemented as part of the program was developed from a careful analysis of students' needs, achievement and related data.

◆ *Student monitoring:* Monitoring students' progress ensures all students receive what they need to achieve success in school. It entails monitoring student achievement data, achievement-related data, and standards- and competency-related data. Collection, analysis and interpretation of student achievement data may be systemic by district or specific to school site, grade, class or individual.

◆ *Closing the gap:* The use of data will drive the program. The needs surface when disaggregated data are analyzed for every student. Data are necessary to determine where the school counseling program is now, where it should be and where it is going to go. Needs are identified discrepancies between the desired results and the results currently being achieved (also referred to as the gap).

Action plans: Two types of action plans, "guidance curriculum" action plans and "closing the gap" action plans are described in the ASCA National Model. Their use ensures a plan is in place for how the program intends to reach every student. Guidance curriculum action plans include: the domain, standard and competency addressed; description of guidance lesson activity;

curriculum or materials to be used; time activity is to be completed; the person(s) responsible for the delivery; and the means of evaluating student success. Closing the gap action plans also describe the data driving the decision addressing this competency.

Use of time: New counselors are often unsure how much time should be spent delivering services in each component area. ASCA's National Model for School Counseling Programs provides a guide to school counselors and administrators for determining the time their program needs to spend in each of the four components of the delivery system.

◆ *Appropriate and inappropriate school counseling program activities:* A comprehensive school counseling program requires counselors to spend the majority of their time in direct service (contact) with students. Therefore, school counselors' duties are limited to program delivery and direct counseling services. Non-school-counseling program tasks are eliminated or reassigned, so school counselors can focus on the prevention and intervention needs of students in their program.

Calendars: Once school counselors determine the amount of time to spend in each area of the delivery system, a master calendar and weekly calendars are developed and published to ensure that students, parents or guardians, teachers and administrators know what is scheduled. This will assist in planning and will ensure active participation in the program. Annual, monthly and weekly calendars ensure planned activities are accomplished.

Accountability
The accountability system answers the question: "How are students different as a result of the program?"

In order to begin to meet the needs of today's students, school counselors must look at individual problems from a systemic perspective. It is no longer enough to only focus on helping students. We must also work to change the system.

Peggy Hines, Ed.D., Indiana State University

Results reports: Results reports, which include process, perception and results data, ensure programs are carried out, analyzed for effectiveness and changed and improved as needed. Sharing these reports with stakeholders serves as an advocacy for the students and the program. Immediate, intermediate and long-range results (impact over time) are collected and analyzed for program improvement.

School counselor performance standards: The school counselor's performance evaluation contains basic standards of

practice expected of school counselors implementing a school counseling program. These performance standards serve as both a basis for counselor evaluation and as a means for counselor self-evaluation.

Program audit: The program audit provides evidence of the programs alignment with ASCA's National Model for School Counseling Programs. The primary purpose for collecting information is to guide future action within the program and to improve future results for students.

> 66*It is my belief that school counselors who work within the structure of a comprehensive program, such as the ASCA National Model for School Counseling Programs, are empowered to be strong advocates for the students and parents they serve.*99
>
> *Norm Gysbers, Ph.D., University of Missouri-Columbia*

Themes

ASCA incorporates the four themes of leadership, advocacy, collaboration and systemic change as part of the framework of The ASCA National Model (The Education Trust, 1997). In the model graphic, the four themes are repeated around the frame to indicate the importance of the school counselors' work within these areas (see page 20). School counselors play a significant part in improving student achievement and are uniquely positioned to be student and systems advocates. School counselors ensure equity and access to rigorous education for every student (Martin & House, 2002).

Leadership: School counselors serve as leaders who are engaged in systemwide change to ensure student success. They help every student gain access to rigorous academic preparation that will lead to greater opportunity and increased academic achievement. Working as leaders, advocates and collaborators, school counselors promote student success by closing the existing achievement gap whenever found among students of color, poor students or underachieving students and their more advantaged peers.

School counselors become effective leaders by collaborating with other professionals in the school to influence systemwide changes and implement school reforms. In this way, school counselors can have an impact on students, the school, the district and the state.

Advocacy: School counselors advocate for students' educational needs and work to ensure these needs are addressed at every level of the school experience. School counselors believe, support and promote every student's goal to achieve success in school. School counselors work proactively with students to remove barriers to learning. As educational leaders, school counselors are ideally situated to serve as advocates for every student in meeting high standards. Advocating for the academic success of every student is a key role of school counselors and places them as leaders in promoting school reform.

School counselors work as advocates to remove systemic barriers that impede the academic success of any student. Through their leadership, advocacy, collaboration, counseling and the effective use of data, school counselors minimize barriers so students have increased opportunities to achieve success in school. These methods promote equity by providing access to rigorous courses and a quality curriculum for every student. Measurable success resulting from these efforts will be the increased numbers of students completing school academically prepared to choose from a wide range of substantial post-secondary options, including college.

Collaboration and teaming: School counselors work with all stakeholders, both inside and outside the school system, to develop and implement responsive educational programs that support the achievement of the identified goals for every student. School counselors build effective teams by encouraging genuine collaboration among all school staff to work toward the common goals of equity, access and academic success for every student. This may include collecting and analyzing data to identify needed changes in the educational program.

School counselors create effective working relationships among students, professional and support staff, parents or guardians and community members. By understanding and appreciating the contributions others make in educating all children, school counselors build a sense of community within the school, which

serves as a platform from which to advocate for every student. In addition, school counselors are a vital resource to parents or guardians, educators and the community agencies. Offering parent or guardian education, information and training in the community, school counselors are essential partners who enhance the educational opportunities of students and their families.

Systemic change: With a schoolwide expectation to serve the needs of every student, school counselors are uniquely positioned to assess the school for systemic barriers to academic success. School counselors have access to critical data about student placement, students' academic success or failure and student course-taking patterns. Collaborating as leaders within the school, counselors have access to quantitative and qualitative data from the school and relevant community sources. They use these data to advocate for every student, ensuring equity and access to a rigorous curriculum, which maximizes post-secondary options.

Systemic change occurs when policies and procedures are examined and changed in light of new data. Such change happens with the sustained involvement of all critical players in the school setting, including and often led by school counselors.

“Students are more important than the system.”

Reese House,
The Education Trust

Foundation

The program's foundation serves as the solid ground upon which the rest of the program is built. The decisions made during this process become the *what* of the program. *What* will every student know and be able to do? Designing a strong foundation requires cooperative effort with parents or guardians, staff and community to determine what every student will receive as a benefit of a school counseling program. During the development stages, stakeholders are consulted when creating the philosophy, mission and overall program focus. The completed foundation is essential to ensuring the school counseling program is an integral part of the total educational program for student success. Elements include beliefs, philosophy, mission statement and ASCA National Standards for student academic, career and personal/social development.

Beliefs and Philosophy

❝If the beliefs are all across the board, that will be reflected programmatically. Philosophy is a clean statement about what we believe in. Beliefs determine behavior.❞

Pat Martin, College Board

Beliefs are personal. Each individual's beliefs must be discussed early in the process of developing a school counseling department philosophy. What we believe about students, families, teachers and the educational process is crucial in supporting successes for every student. Our beliefs are derived from our own background and experiences, and our beliefs drive our behavior.

Dialogue is required to ensure counseling teams and departments explore complex issues from many points of view. Each team member should contribute to the discussion of the following questions:

1. What do we believe about achievement for every student?

2. Do we believe all students can achieve given proper support?

3. Do we believe there are differences in learning styles for students and that children respond differently? How do we react to those responses?

4. What do we believe about the program's ability to provide academic, career and personal/social development for every student?

5. When we look at the school's mission of academic achievement, what responsibility does the school counseling program have to support this mission?

6. What do we believe about educational reform and the school counselor's role in it?

7. What do we believe about the role of parents or guardians, staff and community members within the school counseling program?

After all team members examine their own personal beliefs, they should share them with their teams. Beliefs have no right and wrong answers; they are what drive us to advocate for our students.

Assumptions

The philosophy of a comprehensive school counseling program is often based on certain assumptions. These assumptions will identify and briefly describe the foundation upon which a school counseling program rests. Assumptions give the program its shape and direction, its

nature and structure. As an example, consider the following assumptions:

A school counseling program:
◆ Reaches every student
◆ Is comprehensive in scope
◆ Is preventative in design
◆ Is developmental in nature
◆ Is an integral part of a total educational program for student success
◆ Selects measurable student competencies based on local need in the areas of academic, career and personal/social domains
◆ Has a delivery system that includes school guidance curriculum, individual planning, responsive services and system support
◆ Is implemented by a credentialed school counselor
◆ Is conducted in collaboration with all stakeholders
◆ Uses data to drive program decisions
◆ Monitors student progress
◆ Measures both process and outcome results and analyzes critical data elements
◆ Seeks improvement each year based on results data
◆ Shares successes with stakeholders

Agreeing on program assumptions is the next step. After reviewing the above list of assumptions, school counseling teams should create their own list of assumptions to build into their school counseling program philosophy.

Philosophy

The philosophy is an agreed-upon set of guiding principles individuals follow when implementing the school counseling program (Johnson & Johnson, 2001). It is important that all personnel involved in managing and implementing the program achieve consensus on each belief or guiding principle contained within the philosophy statement. A statement of philosophy is a:
◆ Set of beliefs that motivates program innovations

"The foundation elements clearly delineate desired results and therefore what counselors will contribute."

C.D. Johnson, Ph.D., Retired Counselor Educator

- Set of values visible to all
- Set of principles guiding professional contributions
- Statement of professional conduct
- Statement committing counselors to continuous professional growth
- Source of collective power

When developing a philosophy, school or district teams meet as a group to discuss their beliefs and philosophies. They then use the consensus process to develop the statement of philosophy for their program. At a minimum, a school counseling department philosophy should:

- Indicate an agreed-upon belief system about the ability of all students to achieve
- Address every student
- Address student developmental needs and focus on primary prevention
- Address the school counselor's role as an advocate for every student
- Identify persons to be involved in the delivery or program activities
- Specify who will plan and manage the program
- Use data to drive program decisions
- Define how the program will be evaluated and by whom
- Include ethical guidelines or standards

When developing a philosophy statement, the language and the meaning of the terms must be clear. For example, terms such as manager, administrator and planner may have different connotations to different people on the team. It is important to clearly define who is generally responsible for all program functions such as developing the program, planning activities, monitoring student progress, implementing the program, providing program administration and evaluating data.

> *Even for the states or districts with their own comprehensive, developmental guidance model, ASCA's National Model contributes additional legitimacy, a new vision and rich resources.*
>
> *Dawn Kay, Utah Department of Education*

Sample Philosophical Statement

The counselors in XYZ school believe:
- All students have dignity and worth
- All students have the right to participate in the school counseling program
- All students' ethnic, cultural, racial, sexual differences and special needs are considered in planning and implementing the school counseling program
- All students K-12 shall have access to a full-time, state-certified, master's-degree-level school counselor to deliver the counseling program

And that the XYZ comprehensive school counseling program should:
- Be based on specified goals and developmental student competencies for all students K-12
- Be planned and coordinated by school counseling teams in coordination with other school, parent or guardian and community representatives

- Utilize the many combined resources of the community to deliver programs
- Use data to drive program development and evaluation
- Be evaluated by a counseling supervisor on specified goals and agreed-upon student competencies
- Actively involve counseling team members to monitor students' results

And that all counselors in the XYZ school:
- Abide by the professional school counseling ethics as advocated by the American School Counselor Association
- Participate in professional development activities essential to maintain a quality school counseling program

Mission Statement

One of the essential aspects of the foundation for a school counseling program is the creation of a mission statement, which gives your program overall direction and vision. A mission statement describes the program's purpose and provides the vision of what is desired for every student (Johnson & Johnson, 2001; Gysbers & Henderson, 1998). A school counseling program mission statement aligns with and is a subset of the school or district's mission. Thus, the school counseling program supports the learning environment and at the same time makes unique contributions to meeting students' needs and nurturing their progress. The program's mission statement should be clear, concise and specific as to the program's intent and what the program will contribute.

A mission statement:
◆ Keeps the program's focus on the beliefs, assumptions and philosophy
◆ Establishes a structure for innovations
◆ Creates one vision
◆ Provides an anchor in the face of change

The mission statement content should:
◆ Be written with students as the primary clients
◆ Advocate for the equity, access and success of every student
◆ Be written for every student
◆ Indicate the content and competencies to be learned
◆ Show linkages with the school, school district or state department of education mission statements
◆ Indicate the long-range results desired for all students

Some schools and departments prefer longer mission statements, while others prefer shorter ones. The idea is to create a mission statement everyone can support. The goal is to design a mission statement that is specific, concise, clear and compre-hensive. Figure 3.1 illustrates the system by which school sites gather information to develop the school counseling program mission statement. Sites, districts, states and national organization linkages provide the necessary articulation of information for a cohesive statement, which that is integral to the total educational program. Accordingly, the state comprehensive school counseling program's mission statement is designed to reflect both the ASCA National Model and the state department of education. The school district's school counseling program mission statement is designed to reflect the state school counseling program mission statement and the school district's mission statement. Finally, the site counseling program mission statement reflects the school district school counseling program mission statement and the school site mission statement.

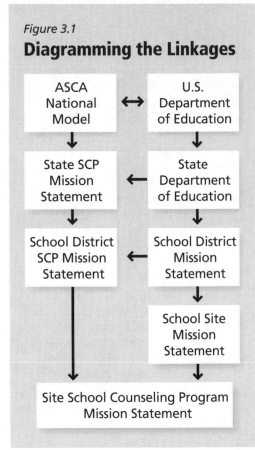

Figure 3.1

Diagramming the Linkages

ASCA National Model ⟷ U.S. Department of Education

State SCP Mission Statement ← State Department of Education

School District SCP Mission Statement ← School District Mission Statement

School Site Mission Statement

Site School Counseling Program Mission Statement

Figure 3.2

Sample Linkage of School Counseling Program Mission Statement

The following example illustrates one district's K-12 school counseling program mission statement. Phrases from the existing district mission along with domains of ASCA's National Standards are the foundation of the school counseling program's mission statement.

XYZ School District
The mission of XYZ Unified School District is to prepare all students academically and socially to contribute at the highest levels as productive members of society, through a partnership of empowered students, educators, parents or guardians and the community responsible for the learning process.

School Counseling Program Mission Statement
The mission of XYZ Unified School District school counseling program is to provide a comprehensive, developmental counseling program addressing the academic, career and personal/social development of all students. School counselors are professional school advocates who provide support to maximize student potential and academic achievement. In partnership with other educators, parents or guardians and the community, school counselors facilitate the support system to ensure all students in XYZ School District have access to and are prepared with the knowledge and skills to contribute at the highest level as productive members of society.

Adapted from Moreno Valley School District, Moreno Valley, CA.

ASCA National Standards for Student Academic, Career and Personal/Social Development

In 1997, the American School Counselor Association published "Sharing the Vision: The National Standards for School Counseling Programs" (Campbell, & Dahir, 1997). This was followed by an implementation guide, "Vision into Action: Implementing the National Standards for School Counseling Programs" (Dahir, Sheldon & Valiga, 1998). ASCA recognizes the significance of these documents and the impact they have had on helping counselors design student competencies within their programs. The ASCA National Model: A Framework for School Counseling Programs incorporates these standards in its foundation. As indicated in the introduction on page 8 however, the

ASCA Task Force participants agreed that the title of the "National Standards for School Counseling Programs" did not accurately reflect the purpose of the "standards." The standards are not for *programs themselves* but rather for students. As such, the nine standards in the three domain areas are actually *content standards for students*, much like states have content standards for students in math and science. They describe what the students should know and be able to do within the educational system. School counselors use them to help students achieve their highest potential. See Appendix, page 81 for ASCA's National Standards for School Counseling Programs.

> **"** The National Model reinforces the importance of linking the National Standards with the process of implementing a comprehensive, developmental, results-based program that is consistent with the current educational reform agenda and responsive to state, district and building-level needs.**"**
>
> *Carol Dahir, Ed.D., New York Institute of Technology*

DOMAINS, STANDARDS, COMPETENCIES AND INDICATORS

The school counseling program facilitates student development in three broad domains to promote and enhance the learning process. Standards for each domain provide guidance and direction for states, school systems and individual schools developing effective school counseling programs. Student competencies define the specific knowledge, attitudes and skills students should obtain, and indicators demonstrate skill acquisition.

Domains

Domains are broad developmental areas including standards and competencies and promote behaviors that enhance learning for all students. The three broad and interrelated domains of student development are:

◆ Academic development
◆ Career development
◆ Personal/social development

Each of these areas of student development encompass a variety of desired student learning competencies, which in turn are composed of specific knowledge, attitudes and skills. Each year school counseling programs set measurable goals in the academic, career and personal/social development domain areas.

The school counseling program reflects the progression of student development throughout the K-12 sequence. The school counselor utilizes a variety of strategies, activities, delivery methods and resources to promote the desired student development. The school counselor's responsibilities include the design, organization, implementation and coordination of the program. By accomplishing this, the goals of the counseling department and the school can be realized.

Content Standards, Competencies and Indicators

Standards and goals are often used synonymously. Standards are those statements providing a description of what students should know and be able to do at the highest level of expectation. Standards specify the level or rate of performance the student will achieve against a particular competency or set of indicators.

Competencies are specific expectations that students achieve in the content standard areas within the academic, career and personal/social development domains.

Indicators describe the specific knowledge, skills or abilities that individuals demonstrate to meet a specific competency.

For example, the following standard, competency and indicators are taken from the academic domain of ASCA's National Standards (Campbell & Dahir, 1997).

DOMAIN: ACADEMIC DEVELOPMENT

STANDARD A:
Students will acquire the attitudes, knowledge and skills that contribute to effective learning in school and across the life span.

Competency A:A1.0
Improve Academic Self-concept

Indicators:
AA:1.1 Articulate feelings of competence and confidence as learners
AA:1.2 Display a positive interest in learning
AA:1.3 Take pride in work and achievement
AA:1.4 Accept mistakes as essential to the learning process
AA:1.5 Identify attitudes and behaviors leading to successful learning

Legend: AA:1.1 = Academic Domain, Standard A, Competency 1 and Indicator 1.

> **"Standards provide guidelines for counselors to develop student outcomes unique for the school."**
>
> *C.D. Johnson, Ph.D., Retired Counselor Educator*

Sample of a Crosswalk Adapted from Connecticut

Figure 3.3
Common Domains

Linking the Common Domains of Student Development with the Connecticut School Counselors Association (CSCA) Goals, ASCA National Standards for School Counseling Programs, National Career Development Guidelines (NCDG) and Competencies and Connecticut's (CT) Common Core of Learning

Domain	CSCA Goals (Strands)	ASCA National Standards	National Career Development Guidelines (Competencies)	CT Common Core (Skills/Competencies)
Academic	Skills for Learning	Standard 1: Students will acquire the attitudes, knowledge and skills that contribute to effective learning in school and across the life span.	Competency 4: Awareness of the benefits of educational achievement Competency 5: Awareness of the relationship between work and learning	• Students will explore the information and arguments from various points of view to think critically and creatively and to solve problems.
	School Success	Standard 2: Students will complete school with the academic preparation essential to choose from a wide range of substantial postsecondary options, including college.	Competency 6: Skills to understand and use career information	• Students will learn how to apply the academic, critical, practical, technical and employability skills needed for success in higher education and the work place and to manage their lives.
	Academics to Life Success	Standard 3: Students will understand the relationship of academics to the world of work and to life at home and in the community.	Competency 7: Awareness of the importance of personal responsibility and good work habits Competency 8: Awareness of how work relates to the needs and functions of society	• Students will actively explore the world of ideas. • Students will demonstrate the effort and persistence needed to be successful in school, work and life.
Career	Investigate Careers	Standard 4: Students will acquire the skills to investigate the world of work in relation to knowledge of self and to make informed career decisions.	Competency 9: Understanding of how to make decisions Competency 10: Awareness of the interrelationship of life roles	• Students will embrace career as a part of their future; acquire employable skills; demonstrate positive attitudes toward work; demonstrate attitudes and habits that are valued in the workplace; explore a range of careers; acquire knowledge of one of CT eight career dusters, explore postsecondary educational opportunities; manage data and use problem-solving and analytical skills to make reasoned decisions.
	Career Success	Standard 5: Students will employ strategies to achieve future career success and satisfaction.	Competency 11: Awareness of different occupations and changing male/female roles	
	Relationship Between School and Work	Standard 6: Students will understand the relationship between personal qualities, education and training and the world of work.	Competency 12: Awareness of the career planning process	
Personal/ Social	Respect for Self and Others	Standard 7: Students will acquire the attitudes, knowledge and interpersonal skills to help them understand and respect self and others.	Competency 1: Knowledge of the importance of self-concept Competency 2: Skills to interact with others	• Students will work and learn independently and collaboratively as part of a team. • Students will gain knowledge and understanding of other cultures. • Students will demonstrate a sense of ethics and take responsibilities for their actions. • Students will be active, constructive members of the larger community. • Students will develop and maintain behaviors that promote lifelong health. • Students will understand the implications of living in a finite world. • Students will understand the role of systems throughout our society. • Students will understand the dynamic nature of society and the universality of change.
	Goal Setting/ Goal-Attainment Skills	Standard 8: Students will make decisions, set goals, and take necessary action to achieve goals.	Competency 3: Awareness of the importance of change and growth	
	Survival and Safety Skills	Standard 9: Students will understand safety and survival skills.		

Ideally, the standards and competencies selected for implementation will be directly aligned with the school's goals. The school's goals in turn must show a relationship with the district as well as the state department of education's goals. Data on goal attainment is reported by the school counseling program to the school and district administration, the advisory council and also to staff, parents or guardians and students, making the program and the progress toward reaching the standards visible to all stakeholders.

ASCA NATIONAL STANDARDS CROSSWALKS

ASCA's National Standards can be aligned with state and national documents to reflect state and local reform initiatives. Standards can also be crosswalked developmentally to ensure all grade levels are addressed. Crosswalking ASCA's National Standards with current school counseling curriculum, activities and student data will show linkages as well as highlight gaps in the programs. In this way, the school counseling program can design activities to ensure students achieve the desired competencies.

Crosswalking ASCA's National Standards with important state, school district and site documents helps show how a school counseling program based on ASCA's National Model aligns with the academic goals of the state and the school.

Crosswalks With State Documents

In some states, standards are aligned across many types of frameworks. For example, ASCA's National Standards may be aligned with:
◆ State education code, laws and regulations
◆ State guidelines for developing a school counseling program
◆ State board of education policies
◆ State academic content standards and frameworks
◆ State accreditation standards
◆ School board policies

Many states have already designed competencies for students to achieve as a result of participation in a school counseling program. Crosswalking offers your program an opportunity to show important linkages between existing curriculum and ASCA's National Standards. The National Career Development Guidelines have been used by many states to develop their programs. See Figure 3.3 for an example of Connecticut's crosswalk aligning the domains, standards, National Career Development Guidelines and the state core competencies. School counselors can use the National Standards as guidelines that may be rewritten to align with district standards or become more measurable.

Crosswalk Content Standards Developmentally

The school counselor initiates and facilitates discussion with the staff to determine which student competencies are the most important to deliver based upon site or district need. The competencies provide direction to assess student growth and progress toward the achievement of the nine ASCA National Standards. Competencies are often identified through the use of needs assessments and data disaggregation. These competencies become a reality check to guide program development and assess student growth and development. Competencies help to identify and monitor knowledge, attitudes and skills that students acquire and demonstrate as a result of participating in a K-12 school counseling program.

Competencies supporting the school mission can be prioritized by the school counselors and school staff for the pur-

Crosswalking ASCA National Standards Developmentally

Figure 3.4

Academic Development Domain (Students will:)

Standard A: Students will acquire the attitudes, knowledge and skills that contribute to effective learning in school and across the life span.	K-2	3-5	6-8	9-12
Competency A1.0 Improve Academic Self-concept				
A:A1.1 • articulate feelings of competence and confidence as learners			✔	✔
A:A1.2 • display a positive interest in learning	✔	✔	✔	
A:A1.3 • take pride in work and achievement	✔	✔	✔	
A:A1.4 • accept mistakes as essential to the learning process			✔	✔
A:A1.5 • identify attitudes and behaviors leading to successful learning	✔			
Competency A2.0 Acquire Skills for Improving Learning				
A:A2.1 • apply time-management and task-management skills			✔	✔
A:A2.2 • demonstrate how effort and persistence positively affect learning			✔	
A:A2.3 • use communications skills to know when and how to ask for help when needed				✔
A:A2.4 • apply knowledge and learning styles to positively influence school performance		✔		
Competency A3.0 Achieve School Success				
A:A3.1 • take responsibility for their actions			✔	✔
A:A3.2 • demonstrate the ability to work independently, as well as the ability to work cooperatively with other students			✔	✔
A:A3.3 • develop a broad range of interest and abilities	✔	✔	✔	✔
A:A3.4 • demonstrate dependability, productivity and initiative				✔
A:A3.5 • share knowledge				✔

pose of having an impact on critical data elements and addressing specific student needs. From a district perspective, some competencies may be critical across all grade levels, while a different school system will emphasize certain competencies at particular grade levels.

There are 122 competencies listed in the ASCA National Standards, and they are not meant to be all-inclusive. No one school or district could possibly cover every competency every year. The standards and the competencies prioritized by the school or district guide the development of the program content in academic, career and personal/social development and are an integral part of individual planning for students, guidance curriculum, responsive services and system support.

Counseling teams meet to discuss and determine which competencies should be covered to meet student needs. Teams may decide that they must prioritize their competencies if they have too many. Some competencies may cross all levels, while others are grade-specific. This is the perfect place for a school counseling program to align itself with the school's academic goals. The school counselor can facilitate the discussion with the staff to clarify which student competencies are the most important ones to assist students in moving toward the school's specific academic goals. Figure 3.4 demonstrates what counselors in one district believed should be covered in Academic Standard A of their school counseling program by grade level. Several academic competencies are selected in grade 6-8, which will

Crosswalking ASCA National Standards with Guidance Curriculum

Figure 3.5 **7th Grade**	Topic of the school guidance curriculum presentation	Violence Prevention	Promotion and Retention	Organization or Test-Taking Skills	Career
	Name of specific lesson or curriculum, production company	XYZ Video and lesson plans	Counselor-generated PowerPoint & handouts	Company XYZ Study Skills & counselor-generated materials	Company XYZ career software programs
ACADEMIC DEVELOPMENT (Students will:)					
Improve Academic Self-concept – STANDARD A					
AA:1.1 • articulate feelings of competence and confidence as learners		·	✔	✔	
AA:1.2 • display a positive interest in learning			✔	✔	✔
AA:1.3 • take pride in work and achievement			✔	✔	✔
AA:1.4 • accept mistakes as essential to the learning process			✔	✔	
AA:1.5 • identify attitudes and behaviors that lead to successful learning			✔	✔	✔
Acquire Skills for Improving Learning – STANDARD A					
AA:2.1 • apply time-management and task-management skills			✔	✔	
AA:2.2 • demonstrate how effort and persistence positively affect learning			✔	✔	✔
AA:2.3 • use communication skills to know when and how to ask for help when needed		✔	✔	✔	
AA:2.4 • apply knowledge and learning styles to positively influence school performance				✔	
Achieve School Success – STANDARD A					
AA:3.1 • take responsibility for their actions		✔	✔	✔	
AA:3.2 • demonstrate the ability to work independently, as well as the ability to work cooperatively with other students				✔	
AA:3.3 • develop a broad range of interest and abilities					✔
AA:3.4 • demonstrate dependability, productivity and initiative			✔	✔	
AA:3.5 • share knowledge					✔

require the team to prioritize its areas of concentration. (See Appendix, page 87 for a sample of ASCA's Developmental Crosswalk Tool.)

Using ASCA's National Standards Developmental Crosswalk (see Figure 3.4), school counselors or teams determine the competency indicators they believe should be addressed by priority at different developmental levels: K-2, 3-5, 6-8, and 9-12.

Crosswalking Content Standards with School Guidance Curriculum

As school counselors implement school guidance curriculum and other activities, it is important to determine which competencies are being addressed. Crosswalks are generally a checklist of standards and competencies related to a scope and sequence of instruction, developmental or academic.

Crosswalking with current guidance curriculum offers counselors an opportunity to evaluate their current program and activities to determine the competencies that are already covered.

Aligning curriculum to the content standards ensures students are acquiring competencies that are integrated and cross-curricular. See figure 3.5 for an example of crosswalking standards with the seventh-grade school guidance curriculum.

Although the example shown on page 36 is from the guidance curriculum, competencies may also be met when counselors provide individual student planning or responsive services.

Evaluating the Crosswalk to Assess What is Missing

After the standards are crosswalked by developmental level and current curriculum or activity, an assessment is made to determine which necessary competencies are not being addressed.

Competencies are representative and are used as a catalyst for the adaptation, modification or adoption of competencies. They are not intended to, nor are they required to, be adopted in a cookie-cutter fashion. Creative and appropriate modification to school site, district or state needs is encouraged, if not recommended.

In summary, the first step (Figure 3.4) crosswalks the standards developmentally and assists the team in determining what they believe "should be." The second step (Figure 3.5) crosswalks current curriculum or activities being delivered and assists the team in determining "what is." In the final step, teams analyze what is missing in the context of their data analysis and make decisions regarding what changes will be made to the program to ensure students receive what they need in the areas of academic, career and personal/social development.

Delivery System

Once the program foundation is completed, focus turns to the method of delivering the program to students. This section describes the activities, interactions and areas in which counselors work to deliver the program. The delivery system (Figure 4.1) and the management system are intertwined throughout this process. The delivery system is the *how* of the implementation process, and the management system addresses the "when, why, by whom and on what authority."

Figure 4.1
Delivery System Components

School Guidance Curriculum
Classroom Instruction
Interdisciplinary Curriculum
Group Activities
Parent Workshops and Instruction

Individual Student Planning
Individual or Small-Group Appraisal
Individual or Small-Group Advisement

Responsive Services
Consultation
Individual and Small-Group Counseling
Crisis Counseling/Response
Referrals
Peer Facilitation

System Support
Professional Development
Consultation, Collaboration and
   Teaming
Program Management and Operation

Adapted from Gysbers, N.C., and Henderson, P. (Eds.) (2000) *Developing and managing your school guidance program (3rd ed.)*, Alexandria, VA: American Counseling Association.

Within the delivery system there are four components: school guidance curriculum, individual student planning, responsive services and system support. All activities included in a school counseling program fit into one of the four areas of the delivery system. The guidance curriculum component provides a vehicle to deliver content standards to every student in a systematic way. The individual student planning component provides all students an opportunity to work closely with parents or guardians to systematically plan, monitor and understand their academic growth and development. The responsive service component responds to the direct, immediate concerns of students and includes, but is not limited to, individual and group counseling, crisis counseling, referrals and consultation with parents or guardians, teachers or other professional specialists. The system support component enables the school counseling program to be effective through a variety of support activities including professional development, consultation, collaboration and teaming, and program management and operations. The system support component also provides appropriate support to other educational programs in the school (Gysbers & Henderson, 2000).

School Guidance Curriculum

The school guidance curriculum component consists of a written instructional program that is comprehensive in scope, preventative and proactive, developmental in design, coordinated by school counselors and delivered, as appropriate, by school counselors and other educators. School guidance curriculum is designed to facilitate the systematic delivery of guidance lessons or activities to every student consistent with the school counseling program's statements of philosophy, goals and student competencies. The guidance curriculum promotes knowledge, attitudes and skills through instruction in three content areas: academic achievement, career development and personal/social growth. The counselor's responsibilities include planning, designing, implementing and evaluating the school counseling curriculum.

School counseling curriculum is planned, ongoing and systematic and includes a clear explanation of the scope and sequence of its units of instruction. It is aligned and crosswalked with ASCA's National Standards and school district's academic goals. The curriculum should include statements of student competencies for each grade level and the indicators that are identified and used in the assessment of student competencies. Guidance curriculum and the related competencies are documented in writing and are based on an assessment of the school counseling program's student population. The knowledge, skills and attitudes are taught using a variety of curriculum or activities and materials. Student mastery of these competencies is assessed using pre-post tests, product creation or activity completion.

Curriculum planning and implementation include the methods and timelines for delivery of units of instruction including, but not limited to, classroom instruction; small-group discussions; presentations to parents or guardians; assemblies; and collaborative activities with teachers, support personnel and other qualified educators.

The curriculum is delivered through such strategies as:

◆ **Classroom instruction:** School counselors provide instruction, team teach or assist in teaching the school guidance curriculum, learning activities or units in the classrooms, the career center or other school facilities.

◆ **Interdisciplinary curriculum development:** School counselors participate on interdisciplinary teams to develop and refine curriculum in content areas. These teams develop school guidance curriculum that integrates with the subject matter. The scope and sequence of the school guidance curriculum may include units delivered through other classroom disciplines.

◆ **Group activities:** School counselors conduct planned small groups outside the classroom to respond to students' identified needs or interests.

◆ **Parent workshops and instruction:** School counselors conduct workshops and informational sessions for parents or guardians to address the needs of the school community and to reflect the student school guidance curriculum.

Individual Student Planning

Individual student planning consists of school counselors coordinating ongoing systemic activities designed to help individual students establish personal goals and develop future plans. School counselors coordinate activities that help all students plan, monitor and manage their own learning as well as meet competencies in the areas of academic, career and personal/social development. Within this component, students evaluate their educational, occupational and personal goals. School counselors help students make the transition from school to school, school to work, or school to higher education or career and technical training. These activities are generally delivered on an individual basis or by working with individuals in small groups or advisement groups. Parents or guardians and other school personnel are often included in these activities. Systematic delivery of individual planning for every student includes a documented strategy for student success.

Individual planning with students is implemented through such strategies as:

◆ **Individual or small-group appraisal:** School counselors work with students analyzing and evaluating students' abilities, interests, skills and achievement. Test information and other data are often used as the basis for helping students develop immediate and long-range plans. In high school, counselors should meet with students yearly to develop and revise students' academic plans.

◆ **Individual or small-group advisement:** School counselors advise students using personal/social, educational, career and labor market information in planning personal, educational and occupational goals. The involvement of students, parents or guardians and the school in planning students' programs that meet their needs is critical.

Examples of topics within the component are:
◆ Test score review, interpretation and analysis
◆ Promotion and retention information
◆ Career decision making
◆ Yearly course selection
◆ Financial aid
◆ Interest inventories

- ◆ Senior exit interviews and surveys
- ◆ Four-year or six-year plans
- ◆ Social skills
- ◆ Test-taking strategies

- ◆ College selection
- ◆ Job shadowing
- ◆ Senior planning appointments
- ◆ Review of behavior plans

Responsive Services

The responsive services component of the school counseling program consists of activities to meet students' immediate needs and concerns. These needs or concerns require counseling, consultation, referral, peer facilitation or information. This component is available to all students and is often student initiated through self-referral. However, teachers, parents or guardians or others may also refer students for assistance. Although school counselors have special training and skills to respond to these needs and concerns, the cooperation and support of the entire faculty and staff are necessary for successful implementation.

66 The counselor is not the program. 99

Paul Meyers, California Department of Education

School counselors offer a range of services along the continuum from early intervention to crisis response to meet students' needs. School counselors consult with parents or guardians, school personnel and other identified parties when developing plans and strategies for facilitating student development. Specific ongoing responsive services provided by school counselors, such as individual and group counseling, crisis management and suicide prevention, are planned and goal-focused. There are written procedures to be used in crisis situations.

Responsive services are delivered through such strategies as:

Consultation: Counselors consult with parents or guardians, teachers, other educators and community agencies regarding strategies to help students and families. School counselors serve as student advocates.

Individual and small-group counseling: Counseling is provided in a small group or on an individual basis for students expressing difficulties dealing with relationships, personal concerns or normal developmental tasks. Individual and small-group counseling helps students identify problems, causes, alternative and possible consequences so they can take appropriate action. Such counseling is normally short term in nature. *School counselors do not provide therapy.* When necessary, referrals are made to appropriate community resources.

Crisis counseling: Crisis counseling provides prevention, intervention and follow-up. Counseling and support are provided to students and families facing emergency situations. Such counseling is normally short term and temporary in nature. When necessary, referrals are made to appropriate community resources. School counselors can provide a leadership role in the district's crisis intervention team process.

Referrals: Counselors use referral sources to deal with crises such as suicidal ideation, violence, abuse, depression and family difficulties. These referral sources may include mental health agencies, employment and training programs, juvenile services and other social and community services.

Peer facilitation: Many counselors train students as peer mediators, conflict managers, tutors and mentors. The techniques of peer mediation and conflict resolution are used to help students learn how to make changes in the way they get along with others. In peer mediation, students are trained in a system to use with fellow students who are having trouble getting along with each other. Mentors and tutors provide additional support.

System Support

System support consists of management activities that establish, maintain and enhance the total school counseling program. School counselors use their leadership and advocacy skills to promote systemic change by contributing in the following arenas:

Professional development: School counselors are involved regularly in updating and sharing their professional knowledge and skills through:

In-service training: School counselors attend school in-service training to ensure their skills are updated in areas of curriculum development, technology and data analysis. They also provide in-service instruction in school counseling curriculum and other areas of special concern to the school and community.

Professional association membership: As the school counseling profession continues to change and evolve, school counselors can maintain and improve their level of competence by attending professional association conferences and meetings.

Post-graduate education: As school counselors are completing post-graduate course work, they are encouraged to contribute to the professional literature.

Consultation, collaboration and teaming: Through consultation, partnering, collaborating and teaming, school counselors provide important contributions to the school system.

Consultation: Counselors must consult with teachers, staff members and par-ents or guardians regularly in order to provide information, to support the school community and to receive feedback on the emerging needs of students.

Partnering with staff, parents or guardians and community relations: This involves orienting staff, parents or guardians, business and industry, civic and social service organizations and community members in the comprehensive school counseling programs through such means as partnerships, newsletters, local media and presentations.

Community outreach: Activities included in this area are designed to help counselors become knowledgeable about community resources, referral agencies, field trip sites, employment opportunities and local labor market information. This may involve counselors visiting local businesses, industries and agencies on a regular basis.

Advisory councils: School counselors are active in serving on community committees or advisory councils, etc. By supporting other programs in the school and community, school counselors gain support for the school counseling program.

District committees: By serving on site and district department, curriculum committees and advisory boards, school counselors assist in generating school-wide and district support.

Program management and operations: This includes the planning and management tasks needed to support

> *Although students are the primary focus, family, staff and community partnerships are essential elements of a school counseling program.*
>
> Carolyn Sheldon,
> Lewis and Clark College

activities conducted in the school counseling program. It also includes responsibilities that need to be fulfilled as a member of the school staff.

Management activities: These include budget, facilities, policies and procedures, research and resource development.

Data analysis: Counselors analyze student achievement and counseling-program-related data to evaluate the counseling program, conduct research on activity outcomes and discover gaps that exist between different groups of students that need to be addressed. Data analysis also aids in the continued development and updating of the school counseling program and resources. School counselors share data and their interpretation with staff and administration to ensure each student has the opportunity to receive an optimal education.

Fair share responsibilities: As team members within the educational system, school counselors perform fair share responsibilities that align with and are equal in amount to the fair share responsibilities provided by other educators on the school site.

For more information on the delivery system, refer to "Developing and Managing Your School Guidance Program (Gysbers & Henderson, 2000).

Management System

The management systems section of ASCA's National Model for School Counseling Programs describes the various organizational processes and tools needed to manage a school counseling program. The management is organized, concrete, clearly delineated and reflective of the school site's needs. Just as school administrators analyze their site data, develop plans of action to meet objectives, abide by a master calendar and provide organizational activities along the way, so too must the school counseling program. This section addresses the *when* (action plan and calendar), *why* (use of data), *who* will implement (management agreement) and *on what authority* (management agreement and advisory council) the school counseling program is delivered. In order to systematically deliver the guidance curriculum and address every student's developmental needs, the school counseling program must be effectively and efficiently managed. Clear expectations and purposeful interaction with administration, teachers, staff, parents and students result in student growth, systemic change and a school counseling program that is integrated into the total educational program. The result is "change" on the part of the student.

The organizational foundation of a school counseling program is built on systems of management, active input of an advisory council, action plans, student monitoring, use of time, calendars, use of data and a precise understanding of school counseling program and non school counseling program responsibilities. Management systems include efforts by administration to support school counselors in delivering the program. Administrators work collaboratively with counselors to analyze student data and develop action plans and implementation timelines. Counselors set up calendars to ensure program implementation, careful monitoring of student progress and maximizing time spent executing the school counseling program.

Management Agreements

Management agreements within the school counseling program ensure effective implementation of the delivery systems to meet students' needs. The entire school counseling staff, including the administrator in charge of school counseling, must make management decisions based on site needs and data analysis. Site principals and administrators must be involved in this important process.

When implementing a comprehensive school counseling program, management system decisions and agreements must be made regarding the organization and assignment of counselors (Johnson & Johnson, 2001). This should be accomplished in consultation with the principal or school counseling administrator prior to the next step in program implementation. It is recommended that:

◆ The school counseling team members and administrator review and discuss data-driven needs for the student population and school site based on data analysis.
◆ The school counseling team decides on a plan of action to meet student needs.
◆ The school counseling team and administrator agree on how students, guidance curriculum and services will be assigned to specific counselors.
◆ The school counseling team produces and presents yearly a draft of the management agreement.
◆ The administrator reviews the management agreement and arrives at consensus with the school counseling team.

Program implementation is predicated on integrating all elements of the school counseling program. (See sample management agreements in the Appendix on pages 101-103.) Organizational plans should include consideration of the following:

◆ How will students be assigned to school counselors to ensure every student has access to the program and acquires the pre-determined competencies? By grade level, alpha breakdown, standards domain, academy or pathway, see any counselor or a combination?
◆ Will counselors choose to specialize in different areas? Who will provide responsive services while other counselors are delivering the scheduled school guidance curriculum? Will the school site implement a "counselor of the day" program so there is always one school counselor available for crisis when others are delivering guidance curriculum?
◆ What amount of time should be spent in delivering guidance lessons, providing individual student planning, delivering responsive services and managing system support? (See page 57.)
◆ Who is responsible for implementation of the various services and specialty tasks?
◆ How will counselors be compensated for work beyond the regular work day?
◆ What budget is available to purchase the necessary materials and supplies to implement the program?

◆ What professional development is needed to support the school counselor or team's ability to provide a comprehensive school counseling program?

◆ How often should the school counseling department meet as a team, with administration, with school staff and with the advisory council?

◆ Who determines how support services for the counseling team will be provided and organized? What role do school counseling assistants, registrars, clerks and volunteers play on the counseling team?

When school counselors and administrators meet and agree on program priorities, implementation strategies and the organization of the counseling department, the entire program runs more smoothly and is more likely to produce the desired results for students.

Advisory Council

An advisory council is a representative group of persons appointed to both advise and assist the school counseling program within a school district. The advisory council reviews the program goals, competencies and results and participates in making recommendations to the school counseling department, principal and superintendent (Johnson & Johnson, 2001). Ideally, advisory council membership reflects the community's diversity. It should include representative stakeholders of the school counseling program: students, parents or guardians, teachers, counselors, administrators, school board members, business and community members. The council should meet twice a year at a minimum.

Advisory council functions can vary. The area of specialization, number of years an educational program has been in existence, program size, community needs and other important items all affect the advisory council's functions. School counselors use data to analyze overall program effectiveness and to make decisions regarding changes in program content and delivery. The advisory council members, using their background and expertise, provide support, input and recommendations for program development and improvement throughout the process. The advisory council, therefore, can be an effective tool to help build an excellent school counseling program. Like any tool, it must be adequately maintained and used properly.

Setting up an Advisory Council

When creating an advisory council, the school counselor must consider two things: stakeholder representation and group size. The advisory council truly represents the school's stakeholders. The broader the representation on the advisory council, the more the group's work will accurately reflect the community's values, concerns, etc. Although broad representation is crucial, the council's size also is an issue. It is important to create an environment that is conducive to informed, constructive discussion. A council with too many members may be ineffective. Generally, a good rule of thumb is to establish a council with a minimum of eight members and a maximum of 20 members.

The first step in forming a viable council is selecting good candidates for membership. The council must be able to function as a communications link between the school counseling program and the various groups to be served: students, parents or guardians, educators, business and the community.

Careful selection of members is critical; screening candidates is a good idea. Certainly appointing members with sincere interests in the counseling program is recommended. Officially invite potential members by letter to serve on the advisory council. Provide a brief explanation in the letter to indicate the amount of time that may be needed and some of the council's purposes. Also give potential members an opportunity to decline.

The advisory council chairperson should have skills in planning and conducting meetings and developing an agenda. Additionally, the chairperson should possess group facilitation skills and consistently demonstrate a positive attitude toward others.

Terms of membership include appointments to definite terms of office serving from one to three years. Provision may be made for staggered replacement so there will always be experienced members serving. When a term has expired, appoint a new council member for a new term.

The person in charge of the council calls the first meeting. Information, in detail, is provided to direct the council's purpose and goals. Along with this information, any reports, other information and data that have been previously collected are included in an information packet to each member. Setting meeting dates and times and other organizational activities should take place at the first meeting. Although the number of meetings may vary, it is suggested that the school counseling advisory council meet at least twice a year to collaborate and give input. At the beginning of the school year, the meeting is held to present the goals and objectives along with the calendar for the school counseling program. At the end of the year, the results gained in the program during the year are shared along with recommendations for program improvement.

Set the advisory council's goals and objectives in advance of selecting advisory council members. It is the responsibility of the educational institution and the counselor involved to let the council know the directions it should take. These goals can be subject to revision as the need might arise. To ensure effectiveness, it is crucial that each advisory council meeting have a specific agenda and goals to be accomplished. Send minutes of previous meetings and an agenda of the upcoming meeting to each member several days in advance.

Use of Data

A comprehensive school counseling program is data-driven. The use of data to effect change within the school system is integral to ensuring that every student receives the benefits of the school counseling program. School counselors must show that each activity implemented as part of the school counseling program was developed from a careful analysis of student needs, achievement and related data. The use of data:

◆ Concretely demonstrates accountability and progress toward goals
◆ Monitors student progress
◆ Creates an urgency for change
◆ Serves as a catalyst for focused action
◆ Engages decision makers, district leaders, school teams, etc. in data-driven decision making
◆ Challenges existing policies, practices, attitudes and mindsets
◆ Exposes evidence of access and equity issues for focused advocacy and interventions
◆ Focuses resources, programs, interventions and strategies where they are needed most
◆ Supports grant proposals
(The Education Trust, 1997)

To create a data-driven school counseling program, school counselors must look at a wide variety of data from several perspectives. Through data analysis, school counselors, administrators, faculty and advisory council members are able to create a current picture of students and the school environment. This picture focuses discussion and planning around students' needs and the school counselor's role in addressing those needs.

MONITORING STUDENT PROGRESS

Using student and school site data to monitor student progress ensures all students receive what they need to achieve school success. School counselors should be proficient in the collection, analysis and interpretation of student achievement and related data. School counselors monitor student progress through three types of data: student-achievement data, achievement-related data, and standards- and competency-related data.

Student-achievement data: Student-achievement data measure students' academic progress. Student-achievement data fields include:

◆ Standardized test data
◆ Grade point averages
◆ SAT and ACT scores
◆ Graduation rate
◆ At or above grade/achievement level in reading, math, etc.
◆ Passing all classes
◆ Promotion and retention rates
◆ Drop out rates
◆ Completion of specific academic programs (i.e., academic honors, college prep, etc.)

Achievement-related data:
Achievement-related data measure those fields the literature has shown to be correlated to academic achievement. These data fields include:

◆ Course enrollment patterns
◆ Discipline referrals
◆ Suspension rates
◆ Alcohol, tobacco and other drug violations
◆ Attendance rates
◆ Parent or guardian involvement
◆ Participation in extracurricular activities
◆ Homework completion rates

Standards- and competency-related data: These data measure student mastery of the competencies delineated in ASCA's National Standards. These data could include:

◆ Percentage of students with four-year plans on file

"Disaggregated data is a powerful tool in the hands of a school counselor who is a student advocate."

Peggy Hines, Ph.D., Indiana State University

- Percentage of students who have participated in job shadowing
- Percentage of students who have set and attained academic goals
- Percentage of students who apply conflict resolution skills

Disaggregate data

To ensure every student achieves high academic standards and masters ASCA's National Standards, it is important to not just look at aggregate, global data from the entire student body but to also disaggregate the data. To disaggregate data, school counselors separate data by variables to see if there are any groups of students who may not be doing as well as others. For example, although a high school counselor might feel good about seeing that 60 percent of all seniors complete four full years of mathematics, she may not be as happy if she sees that 75 percent of white students complete the four years while only 20 percent of students of color complete four years. Disaggregated data often spur change because they bring to light issues of equity and focus the discussion upon the needs of specific groups of students. (See Closing the Gap, page 52.)

Although there are many variables by which data may be disaggregated, the common fields include:
- Gender
- Ethnicity
- Socio-economic status (free and reduced lunch)
- Vocational (multiperiod vocational program track)
- Language spoken at home
- Special education
- Grade level
- Teacher(s)

Program Evaluation Data

It is critically important that school counselors use data to show the school counseling program's impact. To do this, counselors need to evaluate process, perception and results data col-

lected immediately, intermediately and over time (Hatch & Holland, 2001).

Process data: Process data answer the question, "What did you do for whom?" and provide evidence that an event occurred. It is information describing the way the program is conducted and if it followed the prescribed practice (i.e., did school counseling lessons occur in every sixth-grade class on violence prevention? How many students were affected? How many students participated in small group counseling?).

Examples of process data include:
- Held six five-session counseling groups with eight students each on anger management.
- 1,350 sixth- to eighth-grade students received violence prevention school guidance lesson.
- 250 parents or guardians attended a career evening event.
- All high school students were seen individually to prepare an academic plan.

Perception data: Perception data answer the question, "What do people think they know, believe or can do?" These data measure what students and others observe or perceive, knowledge gained, attitudes and beliefs held and competencies achieved. These data are often collected through pre-post surveys, tests or skill demonstration opportunities such as presentations or role play, data, competency achievement, surveys or evaluation forms. Examples of perception data for competency achievement include:
- 100 percent of students in grades 9-12 have completed an academic plan.
- 100 percent of sixth grade students have completed an interest inventory.

Examples of perception data for knowledge gained include:
- 89 percent of students demonstrate knowledge of promotion retention criteria.

66 *Just as data now drive decision-making in schools, so too must data drive the school counseling program.* 99

Peggy Hines, Ed.D., Indiana State University

◆ 92 percent of students can identify the early warning signs of violence.

Examples of attitudes or beliefs data include:

◆ 74 percent of students believe fighting is wrong.
◆ 29 percent of students report feeling safe at school.
◆ 78 percent of students know the name of their school counselor.
◆ 90 percent of the parents or guardians feel they understand college entrance requirements.
◆ 70 percent of eighth grade students understand the relationship between academics and careers.

Results data: Results data answer the "so what" question. The impact of an activity or program is documented through results data. These data show that your program has had a positive impact on students' ability to utilize their knowledge, attitudes and skills to effect behavior change. These data are collected from myriad sources such as attendance rates, number of discipline referrals, grade-point averages, student graduation rates, etc. Examples of results data for behavior change include:

◆ Graduation rates improved by 14 percent.
◆ Attendance improved among seventh grade males by 49 percent.
◆ Discipline referrals decreased by 30 percent.

Data Over Time

To get a true picture of the impact of the school counseling program, it is important to look at data over time. Data can be collected over three different time frames: immediate, intermediate, long range.

Immediate: Data that measure the immediate impact of knowledge, skills and attitudes change as a result of counselor activity or intervention (pre-post tests on student competencies addressed in a classroom unit; four-year plan is completed).

Intermediate: Data collected to measure application of knowledge skills and attitudes over a short period of time (improved test-taking ability, improved classroom behavior after small-group counseling, improved grades this quarter after homework or study skill lessons).

Long range: Schoolwide year-to-year, longitudinal student impact data collected for areas such as student attendance, graduation rates and suspension data.

Data Analysis

School counselors do not have to be skilled statisticians to meaningfully analyze data. Simple percentages can create powerful pictures of what is happening in the school. For example, 72 percent of nonfree and nonreduced lunch students pass the math portion of the state's standardized test, while only 38 percent of the free and reduced lunch students passed. Of the 12 children retained in first grade, 91 percent were boys. Of the 380 school suspensions, 80 percent were for tardiness.

Data Management

Most of the data fields mentioned above are typically available on the students' academic cumulative records or in the school's computerized data system. Student database systems are the most common means by which data are collected and stored. These databases enhance the school counseling program's ability to monitor every student's progress. Although data are important, this does not imply that school counselors are attendance clerks. Schools may employ school counseling assistants or data clerks to assist in the collection and management of this information. Although data collection and analysis takes time, the benefits for students and the school counseling program greatly outweigh these costs. Each school district should decide what is important to be monitored.

❝Our counselors spend endless hours, often unrecognized, serving students and the community. By sharing their results and successes, they no longer hide behind the comfortable veil of modesty; instead, they are celebrated and appreciated as the professionals they are.❞

*Lori Holland,
Moreno Valley Unified
School District*

In addition to school databases, school counselors may find relevant data through additional tools. Two examples are education and career planning folders and student credit card-sized compact discs.

Student education and career planning folders and student portfolios:
These tools may be utilized by the students, parents or guardians and teachers to document and track student progress in the attainment of competencies related to student success. They are also used to showcase student accomplishments and achievements as related to student competencies. They may include the following documentation:

◆ Course selection
◆ Credits earned
◆ Involvement with activities, clubs, service learning, volunteer work
◆ Awards and certificates
◆ Assessments
◆ Interest inventories taken
◆ Letters of recommendation
◆ Student resume
◆ Work experience
◆ Leadership activities

New technology holds even greater promise of efficient and effective monitoring devices. Putting student information on the computer for access by parents or guardians and students, making compact discs or "credit cards" with a magnetic strip that can be accessed for monitoring purposes are only a few of the ideas some schools are exploring. As technological sophistication grows, the formerly daunting task of monitoring student progress promises to become a manageable and valuable strategy. Counselors can't monitor everything, therefore choices must be made depending on what is most appropriate and what is available at the local site.

CLOSING THE GAP

Schools are no longer judged by the accomplishments of their brightest students; they are held accountable for every student's progress. Educational statistics indicate an achievement gap based on geographic location, ethnicity and socioeconomic status (The Education Trust, 2002).

Quality teachers know that not all students learn in the same way or at the same speed. Through the analysis of disaggregated data, they discover which groups of students need additional help and design interventions specifically geared toward those students' needs. For example, to help all students learn to the same high standards, teachers may create differentiated instruction, and schools might institute programs and activities designed to provide extra time and help to those students who need it. These intentional interventions are strategically designed to close the achievement gap.

In the same way, school counselors know that not all students come to school with equal academic and personal/social resources. Disaggregated data help uncover areas where groups of students are having difficulty. Analyzing disaggregated data also uncovers equity and access issues. Once the problem areas are brought to light, it is important to thoughtfully consider those factors that are creating barriers in those areas. School counselors then strategically design programs or activities to help lessen the barriers and begin to close the gap.

The ultimate goal of a school counseling program is to support the school's academic mission. Ensuring academic achievement for every student includes counselor-initiated activities designed to meet the needs of under-served, under-performing and under-represented populations. School counselors do this by examining the student academic achievement data and developing interventions designed to help students succeed. These interventions may take the form of traditional school counseling activities such as classroom presentations and individual or small group counseling. School counselors must also be advocates for students. For example, if data show that Mrs. Smith's students still have a high percentage of discipline referrals after the classroom lesson on conflict resolution, the school counselor may decide to do an extended unit on problem solving for her class. If the data show that the discipline referrals come primarily from a group of five boys in her class who get into fights on the playground, then the counselor may decide to provide guidance curriculum on anger management or create an anger management group for boys.

Although traditional interventions are helpful, school counselors must be advocates for students. As advocates, school counselors work to remove barriers that hinder academic success. They challenge school policies that don't promote stu-dent achievement or equal access to a rigorous curriculum. School counselors advocate for adequate academic support mechanisms, such as tutoring classes. Quality teachers, rigorous curriculum and standards-based assignments are all variables that the literature has shown influences the achievement gap. School counselors also advocate for a school climate where access and support for rigorous preparation for every student is expected. For example, a policy that punishes tardiness with out-of-school suspension does not promote academic achievement and may need to challenged.

The results of these interventions, designed to close the gap, can be documented with student-achievement and achievement-related data. These types of program results move school counseling from the periphery of the school's mission to a position where the educational community views it as critical to student success.

> **ASCA's National Model for School Counseling Programs is the ultimate tool in helping us all to be on the same page, doing the best for students.**
>
> *Mary Pat McCartney,*
> *Bristow Run Elementary*
> *School*

Action Plans

To efficiently and effectively deliver the school counseling program, there must be a plan detailing how the responsible counselor intends to achieve the desired result (Johnson & Johnson, 2001). Action plans are utilized with the planned school guidance curriculum and with closing the gap activities.

The school guidance curriculum plan consists of structured developmental lessons designed to assist students in achieving the competencies (Dahir, Sheldon & Valiga, 1998). The lessons are presented systematically in K-12 through classroom and group activities. The purpose of the school guidance curriculum (as can be reviewed in the Delivery System component) is to provide all students the knowledge and skills appropriate to their developmental level. The curriculum is organized to help students acquire, develop and demonstrate competencies within the three domains.

As mentioned in the Use of Data section, data will drive program decision-making. When data are analyzed for every student, school counseling program gaps and discrepancies surface, and school counselors develop closing the gap plans (Hatch & Holland, 2001). What gaps do the data expose, and what plans must be in place to ensure equity and access to academic achievement for every student? Once the curriculum is agreed to developmentally, it may remain largely similar year to year while the closing the gap activities may change from year to year based on data.

School Guidance Curriculum Action Plans

Guidance curriculum action plans contain:

- Domain and standard to be addressed: academic, career, personal/social
- Student competency addressed
- Description of actual school counseling activity the school counselor or counseling team will provide
- Assurance the curriculum is provided for every student
- Title of any packaged or created curriculum that will be used
- Timeline for completion of activity
- Name of individual responsible for delivery
- Means of evaluating student success using pre-post tests, demonstration of competency or product
- Expected result for students stated in terms of what will be demonstrated by the student
- Indication that the plan has been reviewed and signed by the administrator

Closing the Gap Action Plans

Although the guidance curriculum is for all students, the closing the gap activities address what discrepancies exist in meeting students' needs and their achievement. Each plan contains answers to the following two questions. Why is this competency being addressed? What data drive the need for the activity? These plans contain:

- Data that drive the decision to correlate with a competency
- Domain and standard to be addressed: academic, career, personal/social
- Measurable student competency addressed
- Description of actual school counseling activity the school counselor or counseling team will ensure occurs
- Title of any packaged or created curriculum that may be used
- Timeline for completion of activity
- Name of individual responsible for delivery

Figure 5.1 XYZ Unified School District

XYZ Middle School Guidance Curriculum Action Plan

Year _____

Grade Level	Guidance Lesson Content	ASCA Domain/ Standard	Curriculum and Materials	Projected Start/ Projected End	Projected Number of Students Affected	Lesson Will Be Presented in Which Class/Subject?	Evaluation Methods — How Will the Results Be Measured?	Contact Person
6	Violence Prevention	Personal/ Social C	"XYZ" Violence Lesson	11/01 2/02	450	Social Studies	Pre-Post Tests Number of violent incidents	Jane Doe School Counselor
	Promotion and Retention Criteria	Academic ABC	PowerPoint District Policy	2/02 4/02	450	Language Arts	Pre-Post Tests Number of students retained	Jane Doe School Counselor
	Organizational, Study and Test-taking Skills	Academic ABC	XYZ Study Skills Curriculum	9/01 11/01	450	Language Arts	Pre-Post Tests Scores on Tests	Jane Doe School Counselor

_____   _____   _____   _____
Principal's signature   Date   Date of staff presentation   Prepared by

◆ Means of evaluating student success (what data will you use to show improvement?)

◆ Expected result for students stated in terms of what will be demonstrated by the student

◆ Indication that the closing the gap plan has been reviewed and signed by the administrator

(See the action plan in the Appendix on page 100 for a sample of the closing the gap action plan.)

Use of Time

How much time should school counselors spend delivering services in each component area? New counselors are often unsure. Although some experts assert that it doesn't matter as long as you obtain results for students (Johnson & Johnson, 1997), others maintain that sticking to suggested allocated time distribution does produce the required results. In "Developing and Managing Your School Guidance Program," by Norm Gysbers and Patricia Henderson (2000), the authors encourage school counselors to work with their departments to protect their time so that 80 percent of it is spent in direct service to students, staff and families and the remainder is spent in program management. The following percentages (See Figure 5.2) serve as a guide to school counselors and administrators when determining the time their program needs to spend in each of the four delivery system components.

As a first step to understanding your site's use of time, all the school counselors could keep track of their time and document activities performed throughout their days. This allows school counselors and administrators to determine the amount of time being spent in each of the delivery system components and in non-school-counseling activities. This is especially helpful when first designing the program because it serves to answer the question of "What is" and then provides a forum for the discussion of "What should be?"

In programs with more than one school counselor per site, there is often more flexibility between and among school counselors in determining how much time individual school counselors may spend in the delivery of system components. Keeping in mind that the program percentages are only suggested, the individual time a certain school counselor

---

Figure 5.2

Sample Distribution of Total School Counselor Time

Delivery System Component	Elementary School % of Time	Middle School % of Time	High School % of Time
Guidance Curriculum	35%-45%	25%-35%	15%-25%
Individual Student Planning	5%-10%	15%-25%	25%-35%
Responsive Services	30%-40%	30%-40%	25%-35%
System Support	10%-15%	10%-15%	15%-20%

Adapted from Gysbers, N.C. & Henderson, P. (Eds.) (2000). *Developing and managing your school guidance program,* (3rd ed.), Alexandria, VA: American Counseling Association.

> **"The most powerful tool a counselor can have is a detailed, thorough schedule. Planning your time vs. having time planned for you is vital in reaching all students through the school counseling program."**
>
> *Holly Colonna, Tucson Unified School District*

spends in the delivery of systemic services may vary depending on talents and expertise. School counselors with expertise in group counseling may focus delivering these services, while others may present more school guidance lessons. The time percentages are designed to be programmatic, not counselor specific. Counselors are encouraged to allot times based on program priorities and needs.

A conclusion may also be drawn from use of time information regarding how much time is currently being spent on counseling activities versus non-counseling activities. For example, in one school, 35 percent of the high school counselors' time was being spent on activities other than school counseling. These activities included master schedule building, clerical tasks and the counting and managing of the standardized tests. Following a presentation to district administrators on the results of a time analysis, the administrators decided, and the governing board supported, elimination of the more clerical activities and hired school counseling assistants to help school counselors. Eliminating these activities and providing more clerical help freed school counselors to provide more direct services to students. Again, ASCA recommends school counselors spend a majority of their time in direct service to students.

Figure 5.3

Appropriate Activities for School Counselors

- individual student academic program planning
- interpreting cognitive, aptitude and achievement tests
- counseling students who are tardy or absent
- counseling students who have disciplinary problems
- counseling students as to appropriate school dress
- collaborating with teachers to present guidance curriculum lessons
- analyzing grade-point averages in relationship to achievement
- interpreting student records
- providing teachers with suggestions for better management of study halls
- ensuring that student records are maintained as per state and federal regulations
- assisting the school principal with identifying and resolving student issues, needs and problems
- working with students to provide small- and large-group counseling services
- advocating for students at individual education plan meetings, student study teams and school attendance review boards
- disaggregated data analysis

Inappropriate Activities for School Counselors

- registration and scheduling of all new students
- coordinating or administering cognitive, aptitude and achievement tests
- responsibility for signing excuses for students who are tardy or absent
- performing disciplinary actions
- sending students home who are not appropriately dressed
- teaching classes when teachers are absent
- computing grade-point averages
- maintaining student records
- supervising study halls
- clerical record keeping
- assisting with duties in the principal's office
- work with one student at a time in a therapeutic, clinical mode
- preparation of individual education plans, student study teams and school attendance review boards.
- data entry

Adapted from Campbell, C.A. & Dahir, C.A. (1997). *Sharing the vision: The ASCA national standards for school counseling programs*, Alexandria, VA: American School Counselor Association.

Appropriate and Inappropriate School Counseling Program Activities

A school counseling program recommends counselors spend most of their time in direct service to and contact with students. Therefore, school counselors' duties are focused on the overall delivery of the total program through guidance curriculum, individual student planning and responsive services. A small amount of their time is devoted to indirect services called system support. Prevention education is best accomplished by implementing school guidance curriculum in the classroom and by coordinating prevention education pro-grams such as the conflict resolution and anti-violence programs at school sites. Eliminate or reassign certain inappropriate program tasks, if possible, so school counselors can focus on the prevention needs of their program. Figure 5.3 represents a comparison between the two similar types of activities and serves as a helpful teaching tool when explaining the school counseling program activities. For example, when considering discipline, counseling students who have discipline problems is the role of the school counselor while performing the disciplinary action itself is the role of the administrator.

Calendars

School counselors develop and publish a master calendar of school counseling events to ensure students, parents or guardians, teachers and administrators know what and when school counseling activities are scheduled and when and where activities will be held. Calendars also assist with planning, ensuring program participation.

The use of a school counseling program calendar aligned with the school site calendar facilitates staff, parents or guardians, student and community involvement as partners in students' education. The calendar establishes a site schedule for the school and counseling program activities. As the program grows and multiple activities are developed, a calendar validates the important support the school counselor program provides students, parents or guardians, teachers and administrators. A well-developed calendar that is complete, timely and colorful can be a powerful public relations booster. Time and thought on how the calendar will be formatted, consistency in the timing and distribution methods, attractiveness of the design, color and detail produce a useful tool. An effective calendar invites others to acknowledge and participate in the school counseling program activities (Henderson & Gysbers, 1998; Johnson & Johnson, 2001; Myrick, 2003).

A school counseling program is balanced in two ways:
- In the delivery system (i.e. school guidance curriculum, individual student planning, responsive services and system support)
- In the use of time spent delivering the components

Calendars can:
- Identify grade levels, dates and activities
- Be published and distributed to appropriate persons: students, staff, parents or guardians and community
- Be posted on a weekly or monthly basis
- Be compared to locally established goals for time spent in the delivery of system components
- Be utilized to allocate time for data analysis and program evaluation

- Be used when designing and determining system priorities
- Be shared with the principal as an indicator of leadership, advocacy and foresight in the school counselor's professional approach

Annual calendar

The yearly calendar is a way for school counselors to identify the school counseling program priorities and their commitment to them. Ideally, the calendar is located in several prominent places such as the department bulletin board, school or student bulletin boards, classroom bulletin boards, administrative offices, parent or guardian center, career center, student store and other sites used to communicate school events. It may also be submitted to the local newspaper, the student newspaper and the school counseling department's website to increase the program's visibility. The student support calendar might include relevant school activities for families, such as back to school night, open house, parents or guardian-teacher meetings, standardized tests dates, parents or guardian, student and teacher conferences, planned school counseling classroom lessons, career or college nights, evening meetings for reviewing study skills or other opportunities provided through the school and the community, as well as the student support program.

Many schools provide a yearly schedule of school activities that can be coordinated with other events with all relevant dates and times noted on the student support calendar. The school counseling program calendar:

- Increases visibility of the student support program and other related educational activities
- Provides focus on events or activities of value for the students, parents or guardians and staff
- Increases communication within the school and home about schedules and program activities
- Encourages the student, family, department and school to plan ahead for important student support functions
- Establishes an organizational pattern of highlighting and valuing student support opportunities
- Reserves the use of the facility hosting the events or activities
- Reinforces the importance of student participation in student support-related activities

Monthly calendar

The monthly calendar is maintained and circulated to highlight the specific activities and events for each month throughout the school year and into the summer. Print the monthly calendar in a distinctive color and distribute it to all teachers for their classroom bulletin boards. Be sure to remind teachers that they are invited to participate and to encourage student participation or observance of upcoming events. Mail the calendar to parents or guardians as well. Schedule classroom guidance lessons on a monthly basis, such as one grade level per month for four to six lessons.

Weekly calendar

The weekly calendar is not a master schedule but a fluid road map that is somewhat flexible due to crisis or immediate student needs. In addition to classroom lessons, group counseling and individual planning, build in data analysis, collaboration and advocacy into the schedule to allow for some flexibility.

Accountability System

Accountability and evaluation of the school counseling program are absolute necessities. School counselors and the school counseling program must answer the question, *"How are students different as a result of the school counseling program?"* Now more than ever, school counselors are challenged to demonstrate the effectiveness of their programs in measurable terms. School counselors must collect and use data that support and link the school counseling programs to students' academic success.

Results Reports

Results reports help answer the question, "How are students different as a result of the program?" (Johnson & Johnson, 2001).

Results reports ensure programs are carried out, analyzed for effectiveness and changed and further improved as needed. The student results data are collected for activities outlined in the actions plans. The goal is to show change in student behavior and student learning. Sharing these results with stakeholders serves as an advocacy for students and the program. The school counseling program supports every student's academic achievement. It seeks to assist every student in the mastery of competencies designed to foster academic, career and personal/social development. In addition, the program, through the advocacy and leadership of school counselors, discovers and facilitates the removal of barriers to learning.

Data collection provides the school counseling program with the information needed to evaluate the program as it relates to students' progress. How are students different as a result of the program, lesson, activity? Data collection occurs both before and after the school counseling activity. The data indicate what worked and what didn't and clarify what needs to be changed or improved.

Programs can be scrutinized for effectiveness during the implementation process. Data are collected at three different intervals. Short-term data provide an immediate evaluation of the activity process on student behavior or student learning. Intermediate data collection occurs over a longer period of time as a benchmark or indication of progress toward the goal. Long-term data collection occurs over an extended period of time and measures the activity's overall results for students. For example, if data indicate poor graduation rates, school counselors may plan classroom lessons and follow-up small-group interventions. Students may take pre and post tests (short-term data) to assess if they

gained the knowledge of what is needed to graduate; progress reports and grading periods indicate the progress toward passing required courses (intermediate data); and a measure of graduation rates would indicate if students changed as a result of the school counseling program (long-term data).

Figure 6.1 shows a results report for a closing the gap activity. (See page 108 in the Appendix for a copy of the guidance curriculum results report.)

Collecting and analyzing results is key to assessing program effectiveness after the activity is completed; we must be able to know where students are as a result (Myrick, 2003). These results can be powerful advocacy tools when promoting the school counseling program.

Figure 6.1 XYZ Unified School District

XYZ Middle School Results Report

Year _____

Counselor	Target Group	Curriculum and Materials	Type of Service (Delivered in what manner?)	Start Date/ End Date	Process Data (Number of students affected)	Perception Data* (Pre and post test competency attainment or student data)	Results Data* (How did the student change as a result of the lesson?)	Implications (So what do the data tell you?)
Berry	8th Grade—64 students in danger of being retained at the end of Trimester 1	Promotion retention guidance lessons "XYZ" Study Skills Video Series	Academic Counseling Groups Peer Mentoring	Sept. 2002 June 2003	64	*Immediate* 99% correct on post-test knowledge of promotion information.	*Intermediate* 46 (72%) demonstrated improvement in GPA from Trimester 1 to Trimester 3. *Long term* 85% of at risk students showed improvement in GPA from Trimester 1 to Trimester 2.	Excellent academic improvement. Re-evaluate the curriculum used. Participants in the academic support groups may need further encouragement from other resources such as adult mentors.

Principal's signature _____   Date _____   Prepared by _____

* Attach data, examples and documentation

The results report serves as a tool for:
◆ Ensuring the program was carried out as planned
◆ Ensuring every student was served
◆ Ensuring developmentally appropriate materials were used
◆ Documenting the program's process, perception and results data
◆ Documenting the program's immediate, intermediate and long-range impact
◆ Analyzing the program effectiveness
◆ Sharing the program's successes
◆ Improving the program
◆ Advocating for systemic change in the school system

The results reports for school counseling curriculum may include the following:
◆ The grade level served
◆ Lesson content areas
◆ Curriculum or materials used
◆ Process data such as the number of school counseling lessons delivered and in what subject area
◆ Process data such as the number of students served
◆ Short-term perception data such as pre-post tests of knowledge gained
◆ Intermediate and long-term results data such as the impact on behavior, attendance or achievement
◆ The implications of the results on the counseling program

> **Results are not about what counselors do. Results are about what students do.**
>
> *C.D. Johnson, Ph.D., Retired Counselor Educator*

Impact of the School Counseling Program Over Time

Demographics, graduation and college-going rates, discipline and attendance data, test scores and other standardized sources of statistical information capture the overall view of student progress. Comparing data over time offers long-term information reflecting trends in student improvement or areas of concern, which become concentration areas for improvement (Johnson & Johnson, 2001).

The impact-over-time form (see Figure 6.2 and Appendix, page 109) serves as a summary sheet listing baseline and change data over time. This allows a review of data trends in all domain areas: academic, career, personal/social. It gives the counseling staff a tool to review overall student progress and provides a review of the comprehensive program for the school site or district. Using the schoolwide results report gives counselors and administrators the big picture and serves as a catalyst for systemic change.

Although school counselors may see immediate results in attendance, behav-ior and academic achievement, school-wide systemic change requires data that tell the larger story and present an over-all schoolwide evaluation of student progress. Additionally, community demographics can change, and this will be reflected in the student population. As student populations change, results will change. Tracking this information over time helps sites evaluate and alter programs based upon local need.

The school may already have a school report card full of valuable information. This is an excellent beginning source for reporting the site's academic, career and personal/social development and progress over time. The reported information depends on school or school district priorities and may include such information as:

◆ Demographic data
◆ Attendance data
◆ Suspension and expulsion rates
◆ Behavioral referrals
◆ Promotion and retention rates
◆ Graduation rates
◆ Standardized testing results

Figure 6.2

Results Report: Impact Over Time

SAMPLE

ACADEMIC Standard A – acquire knowledge attitude and skill leading to effective learning	2000-2001	2001-2002	2002-2003	2003-2004
Attendance data	93.4%	94.2%	95%	
Retention rates	5.4%	5.1%	4.5%	
% of students of color taking AP classes	1%	3%	5%	

Documenting baseline data prior to programmatic restructuring provides ready, necessary information for data-based decision making. Each year data are charted indicating growth or change in the areas of concern. The data are analyzed in relation to progress made toward the school-wide mission and achievement goals. Accountability charts are easy to read and easy to use to convey what has changed over time (see Figure 6.2). Noticing trends over time invites reflection, discussion and participation by all stakeholders in assessing the program for continual program evaluation and improvement.

The impact-over-time form minimally contains the following:
◆ Student demographics: Enrollment data, gender, ethnicity, grade levels and languages
◆ Academic achievement: Standardized test scores, grade-point averages, dropout rates, graduation rates
◆ Career development: Students enrolled in work experience, job shadowing
◆ Personal/social development: Climate survey results, substance use and abuse statistics, attendance data and suspension and expulsion data
◆ Parents or guardian involvement: Parents or guardian attendance at evening activities, parent workshops and conferences

The information in the school profile is extremely valuable for all school counseling personnel. Collecting these data at the beginning creates a baseline from which to measure program results. Yearly updates assess both program progress and impact. The information reveals areas of strength and weakness and growth or loss in overall program success. It is also a convenient tool for sharing systemic change, programmatic successes and needs.

School Counselor Performance Standards

School counselor performance standards align with the ASCA National Model and contain basic standards of practice expected from counselors. Personnel delivering the school counseling program are evaluated in the areas of program implementation, program evaluation and professionalism. All too often, school counselors are evaluated using an instrument designed for teachers or resource professionals. These school counselor standards accurately reflect the unique training of school counselors and their responsibilities within the school system. Although used for performance evaluation, the standards are also an important tool in the school counselor's own self-evaluation and will help focus personal and professional development plans. It is suggested that school counselors and administrators work within their individual systems to design appropriate evaluation and/or appraisal tools that meet their district governing board and bargaining unit policies. It is recommended that administrators evaluate school counselors every year. An evaluation should include individual comments as well as a rating system for how well the school counselor is meeting required performance standards.

School counselor standards are:
Standard 1: Program organization
Standard 2: School guidance curriculum delivered to all students
Standard 3: Individual student planning
Standard 4: Responsive services
Standard 5: Systems support
Standard 6: School counselor and administrator agreement
Standard 7: Advisory council
Standard 8: Use of data
Standard 9: Student monitoring
Standard 10: Use of time and calendar
Standard 11: Results evaluation
Standard 12: Program audit
Standard 13: Infusing themes

Standard 1: The professional school counselor plans, organizes and delivers the school counseling program

1.1 A program is designed to meet the needs of the school.

1.2 The professional school counselor demonstrates interpersonal relationships with students.

1.3 The professional school counselor demonstrates positive interpersonal relationships with educational staff.

1.4 The professional school counselor demonstrates positive interpersonal relationships with parents or guardians.

Standard 2: The professional school counselor implements the school guidance curriculum through the use of effective instructional skills and careful planning of structured group sessions for all students.

2.1 The professional school counselor teaches school guidance units effectively.

2.2 The professional school counselor develops materials and instructional strategies to meet student needs and school goals.

2.3 The professional school counselor encourages staff involvement to ensure the effective implementation of the school guidance curriculum.

Standard 3: The professional school counselor implements the individual planning component by guiding individuals and groups of students and their parents or guardians through the development of educational and career plans.

3.1 The professional school counselor, in collaboration with parents or guardians, helps students establish goals and develop and use planning skills.

3.2 The professional school counselor demonstrates accurate and appropriate interpretation of assessment data and the presentation of relevant, unbiased information.

Standard 4: The professional school counselor provides responsive services through the effective use of individual and small-group counseling, consultation and referral skills.

4.1 The professional school counselor counsels individual students and small groups of students with identified needs and concerns.

4.2 The professional school counselor consults effectively with parents or guardians, teachers, administrators and other relevant individuals.

4.3 The professional school counselor implements an effective referral process with administrators, teachers and other school personnel.

Standard 5: The professional school counselor provides system support through effective school counseling program management and support for other educational programs.

5.1 The professional school counselor provides a comprehensive and balanced school counseling program in collaboration with school staff.

5.2 The professional school counselor provides support for other school programs.

Standard 6: The professional school counselor discusses the counseling department management system and the program action plans with the school administrator.

6.1 The professional school counselor discusses the qualities of the school counselor management system with the other members of the counseling staff and has agreement.

6.2 The professional school counselor discusses the program results anticipated when implementing the action plans for the school year.

Standard 7: The professional school counselor is responsible for establishing and convening an advisory council for the school counseling program.

7.1 The professional school counselor meets with the advisory committee.

7.2 The professional school counselor reviews the school counseling program audit with the council.

7.3 The professional school counselor records meeting information.

Standard 8: The professional school counselor collects and analyzes data to guide program direction and emphasis.

8.1 The professional school counselor uses school data to make decisions regarding student choice of classes and special programs.

8.2 The professional school counselor uses data from the counseling program to make decisions regarding program revisions.

8.3 The professional school counselor analyzes data to ensure every student has equity and access to a rigorous academic curriculum.

8.4 The professional school counselor understands and uses data to establish goals and activities to close the gap.

Standard 9: The professional school counselor monitors the students on a regular basis as they progress in school.

9.1 The professional school counselor is accountable for monitoring every student's progress.

9.2 The professional school counselor implements monitoring systems appropriate to the individual school.

9.3 The professional school counselors develops appropriate interventions for students as needed and monitors their progress.

Standard 10: The professional school counselor uses time and calendars to implement an efficient program.

10.1 The professional school counselor uses a master calendar to plan activities throughout the year.

10.2 The professional school counselor distributes the master calendar to parents or guardians, staff and students.

10.3 The professional school counselor posts a weekly or monthly calendar.

"Setting the standards into action was the beginning of the process that has expanded to this next step, The ASCA National Model: A Framework for School Counseling Programs. The best thinking and leadership have formulated this model, and we have only begun. I ask 'What is next?' As we transform and evolve our profession to the pinnacle."

Brenda Melton, San Antonio Independent School District & ASCA President 2002-2003

10.4 The professional school counselor analyzes time spent providing direct service to students.

Standard 11: The professional school counselor develops a results evaluation for the program.

11.1 The professional school counselor measures results attained from school guidance curriculum and closing the gap activities.

11.2 The professional school counselors works with members of the counseling team and with the principal to clarify how programs are evaluated and how results are shared.

11.3 The professional school counselor knows how to collect process, perception and results data.

Standard 12: The professional school counselor conducts a yearly program audit.

12.1 The professional school counselor completes a program audit to determine the degrees to which the school counseling program is being implemented.

12.2 The professional school counselor shares the results of the program audit with the advisory council.

12.3 The professional school counselor uses the yearly audit to make changes in the school counseling program and calendar for the following year.

Standard 13: The professional school counselor is a student advocate, leader, collaborator and a systems change agent.

13.1 The professional school counselor promotes academic success of every student.

13.2 The professional school counselor promotes equity and access for every student.

13.3 The professional school counselor takes a leadership role within the counseling department, the school setting and the community.

13.4 The professional school counselor understands reform issues and works to close the achievement gap.

13.5 The professional school counselor collaborates with teachers, parents and the community to promote academic success of students.

13.6 The professional school counselor builds effective teams by encouraging collaboration among all school staff.

13.7 The professional school counselor uses data to recommend systemic change in policy and procedures that limit or inhibit academic achievement.

The Program Audit

A comprehensive school counseling program is multifaceted and designed with continuous evaluation and modification in mind. Audits serve to set the standards for the school counseling program. (See Figure 6.3.) The program audit is a tool aiding school counselors in the breakdown and analysis of each program component (Arizona Department of Education, 2002; Johnson & Johnson, 2001; Bowers & Colonna, 2001). Once completed, the audit indicates implementation areas that will be improved or enhanced. The program audit provides evidence of the program's alignment with ASCA's National Model for School Counseling Programs. The primary purpose for collecting this information is to guide future actions within the program and to improve future results for students. The audit aligns with and includes all national model program components.

Figure 6.3

Program Audit

The program audit is used to assess the school counseling program in comparison with ASCA's National Model for School Counseling Programs. Audits are first consulted when a school counseling program is being designed and then yearly to appraise the progress of the program development. Using the findings of both program implementation and results, strengths and weaknesses are determined and goals are created for the following school year.

School _____ Date _____

FOUNDATION

I. PHILOSOPHY
The philosophy is a set of principles that guide the development, implementation and evaluation of the school counseling program.

CRITERIA	None	In Progress	Completed	Implemented	N/A
1.1 A statement of philosophy has been written for the school counseling program.					
1.2 Indicates an agreed-upon belief system about the ability of every student to achieve.					
1.3 Addresses EVERY student's right to a school counseling program.					

(See page 110 in the Appendix for a complete sample of a program audit form.)

School counselors evaluate each criterion as:

None: meaning not in place

In progress: perhaps begun, but not completed

Completed: but perhaps not as yet implemented

Implemented: fully implemented

Not applicable: for situations where the criteria does not apply

Ideally, the program audit is conducted annually in the spring. After completing the audit, analyze responses to determine the following:

◆ Major strengths of the program
◆ Items in greatest need of strengthening
◆ Short-range goals for improvement
◆ Long-range goals for improvement

As school counselors begin to revise their program and work toward completing and implementing the specific criterion, they may chose to either present each section to the administration for acceptance as completed or complete the entire program before presenting it for acceptance in its entirety. This decision is made locally. Regardless of approach, share program results with the advisory council. The results should drive the program goals, training and behavior for the following year.

Implementation

Administrator support is necessary to ensure effective implementation of the school counseling program. The entire school counseling staff, including the administrator in charge of the school counseling department, collaborates to make management decisions. Site principals and administrators are involved in this process for several important reasons:

- Administrators are the school leaders who understand the school's direction and needs.
- Administrators who meet regularly with the counseling staff to discuss the school's mission and the counseling program are critical links in supporting the school's mission and meeting student needs.
- Without administrator support, school counseling programs may strive, but they will not thrive.
- An involved and supportive administrator is one of the school counseling program's best advocacy tools.
- Administrators work collaboratively with counselors to create a systemic and interdependent approach to improve student academic achievement.
- Both school counselors and administrators are especially alert to and responsible for the needs of every student, including those who are under-served (Van Zandt, Burke & DeRespino, 1998).

Pre-conditions

To support the school counseling program it is helpful to have the following:

Program
- Every student, parent or guardian, teacher and other recipient of the

school counseling program has equal access to the school counseling program.
- The program operates in a supportive work environment and has an adequate budget and

School counseling is a journey. If you don't know where you are going you will end up somewhere else.

Stan Maliszewski, Ph.D., University of Arizona

school counseling materials.

◆ The school counselor works cooperatively with parents or guardians, teachers and community partners and follows ASCA and local policies regarding counseling with students.

◆ School administrators understand and support the program's priorities and demands.

◆ The state departments of education provide leadership and technical assistance as the schools in each state implement a school counseling program.

Staff

◆ School counselors hold a valid school counselor certification from their state.

◆ School counselor responsibilities are clearly defined by the program to make maximum use of the school counselor's expertise.

◆ The student-to-counselor ratio is appropriate to implement the designed program. ASCA recommends a ratio of at least one school counselor to every 250 students.

◆ All staff members accept responsibility for the infusion of school counseling standards and competencies into the program.

◆ School counselors are members of their state and national professional associations.

Budget

◆ A school counseling department budget is established to support program needs and goals.

◆ Budgets similar to those of other departments are established at the local or district level.

◆ Local, state and federal funds are made available to support the program's goals.

Materials, Supplies and Equipment

◆ Materials are relevant to the program and appropriate for the community.

◆ The school counselor consults with the advisory committee and the local board policy concerning the evaluation and selection of program materials.

◆ Materials, supplies and equipment are easily accessible and of sufficient quantity to support the program.

◆ All school counselors have locking file cabinets, private telephone lines and computers with Internet access in their offices.

Facilities

◆ All facilities are easily accessible and provide adequate space to organize and display school counseling materials.

◆ The school counselor has a private office that is designed with consideration of the student's right to privacy and confidentiality.

◆ As available, access is provided to facilities for meeting with groups of students.

Technology

◆ School counselors use technology daily in their work, including the Internet, word processing, student database systems and presentation software.

◆ School counselors use technology to help students perform career and advanced educational searches and create online portfolios.

◆ School counselors use data regarding their school population to work with the principal, teachers and the advisory council in making recommendations to improve academic achievement.

◆ School counselors receive yearly training in all areas of technology advancement and updates.

◆ School counselors use technology in the planning, implementation and evaluation of the school counseling program.

◆ School counselors use technology as a tool to gather, analyze and present data to drive systematic change.

Steps to Implementation

When schools and districts decide to adopt ASCA's National Model for School Counseling Programs, there are five steps of change that departments and districts will go through: planning the program, building the foundation, designing the delivery system, implementing the program and making the program accountable.

The steps outlined below will help manage the transition to a school counseling program. During the transition, school teams may want to consider these questions:

- Where are we now?
- Where do we want to be?
- Who are our partners?
- How do we get to where we want to be?
- How will we know when we are there?

1. Planning the Program

The planning phase starts with the decision to align with ASCA's National Model for School Counseling Programs. As schools and districts work to initiate the change, it is essential that everyone is working toward the same goal.

A. Securing Commitment
- First, read ASCA's National Model for School Counseling Programs.
- Determine and agree that change is necessary.
- Understand the conditions necessary for effective change.
- Expect some resistance to change.
- Appreciate and accept the challenges involved.
- Facilitate communication between counselors and administrators.
- Follow ASCA's Code of Ethics.

B. Getting Organized
- Form a cadre of school counselors and staff members to work as a program development team.
- Obtain formal approval to proceed with the development of a school counseling program based on ASCA's National Model for School Counseling Programs.
- Develop a timeline for program development.
- Compile your own comprehensive school counseling program manual as you go through the stages of implementation.

C. Assessing Your Current Program in comparison to ASCA's Model
- Use the ASCA program audit to identify components and elements in place and to be developed.
- Identify current counseling functions, activities and services.
- Review activities in light of the delivery system.
- Conduct a counselor use-of-time analysis.
- Prepare a report of the use-of-time analysis.
- Identify how current resources are used, who is served by the current program and areas for program improvement.

2. Building your Foundation

A. Assess Needs of the School and District
- Use data from surveys for teachers, parents or guardians and students to identify needs.
- Use school achievement and related data including attendance, drop-out rates, graduation rates, college attendance rates.

As school counselors learn and implement the National Model, students will become successful academically, in personal/social development and have a good understanding of career opportunities as they face the world of work.

Pam Gabbard, Ballard County Elementary School & ASCA President 2001-2002

- Identify current program strengths and areas where improvement is needed.

B. Commit to Program
- Discuss beliefs about students and learning, your philosophies and mission.
- Write the program philosophy.
- Write the program mission statement.

C. Select Competencies
- Identify student standards, competencies and indicators that address the need areas.
- Identify a developmental continuum of goals and competencies to be achieved over time.
- Determine program priorities based on data and school needs.
- Identify desired student standards, competencies and indicators by grade level or by domain.

3. Designing the Delivery System

After creating a philosophy, designing a mission statement and determining competencies for the school counseling program, priorities are identified and corresponding percentages of counselor time is allocated to each component in the delivery system. In addition, a counselor's job description that reflects 100 percent guidance activities would also be developed.

The program must be clear, purposeful and presented in a manner that can be easily understood by all who are involved in the program.

- Identify specific counseling elements for each program component based on the time percentages chosen.

- Develop action plans.
- Identify the curriculum to be used.
- Determine data you will collect when implementing the program (process, perception results, immediate, intermediate and long term).
- Decide who will do what and when.
- Rally administrative support.

4. Implementing the Program

In this phase, the school or district school counseling program is put into operation. The most important aspect of this phase is to have the official approval or adoption from the school district governing board. This requires the board to have a working knowledge of the program and to be prepared to assume ownership and support all aspects of the program.

A. Setting up the program
- Establish the budget for the program.
- Consider the pre-conditions mentioned in the model.
- Complete the management agreement forms.

B. Working in the program
- Develop a master planning calendar for the program at all levels.
- Determine school counselor target time allocations based upon your program's design.
- Develop a weekly and monthly planning calendar based on the master calendar.
- Conduct professional development activities.
- Launch the program by implementing guidance curriculum for each grade level.
- Select at least one closing the gap activity to implement and measure.

C. Promoting the school counseling program
- Develop a brochure.
- Present the program to the school site staff.
- Develop a Web site for school counseling department.
- Present the program to the governing board for official approval.

5. Making the Program Accountable

In this phase, the school implementation team or district will determine how successful the program adoption has been. When the program is fully implemented, an evaluation to determine the program's effectiveness is conducted and shared with the advisory council. Evaluation provides the information to ensure that there is a continuous process to measure the results of the school counseling program.

A. Monitor program results
- Develop program results reports.
- Develop evaluation standards and indicators to establish the degree to which program is in place.
- Revisit your audit to determine areas of improvement and areas requiring more attention.
- Reflect on the results when making decisions for program

adjustment and improvements.
- Assess how the counseling team is working together.

B. Monitor counselors' growth and performance
- Encourage and promote counselor professional growth.
- Develop a job description.
- Develop and use appropriate forms to supervise and evaluate counselors on job performance.

C. Monitor students' progress
- Assess student mastery of selected student competencies.
- Assess impact of school counseling program on the selected goals in the action plan (process, perception and results data).
- Assess the impact of the school counseling program effectiveness in the areas of attendance, behavior and academic achievement.
- Prepare and share the results report with the school site, parents or guardians and school board.

(Adapted from Michigan School Counselor Association, 1997 & Missouri Department of Elementary and Secondary Education, 1998)

> **❝The National Model empowers school counselors to place themselves at the front and center of the restructuring process in their school systems by advocating for high aspirations and high expectations for every student. School counselors can lead the conversation to more critical data elements in a positive direction.❞**
>
> *Carol Dahir, Ed.D., New York Institute of Technology*

Impact of Program Transformation

In a recent school counselor survey conducted in the Moreno Valley Unified School District, Moreno Valley, Calif., that followed the process of transforming its school counseling program, the following comments were collected:

How has your program changed?
"We provide more direct services to

students than ever before."
"We have more accountability for how we impact students."
"We now have fewer clerical responsibilities as a result of administrators understanding our role."
"We have been supported to receive more counselor staff development."

"We provide more guidance lessons – at all levels."

"Our work is more student-focused, not administrator-focused."

"The staff is more aware of what we do."

What were your obstacles?

"Changing our philosophy."

"Facing fear of failure (some of us had never done classroom guidance presentations)."

"Needing more pre-post tests – now we have created our own and shared with each other."

"Learning what results-based really means."

"Some of our "old" counselors needed to adjust and get on board."

"I felt guilt initially when I stopped enabling my administrators when doing non-school counseling activities."

"It was hard to risk presenting to staff the first time – to seek their support."

"I had to learn to trust my team."

What worked best?

"The action plans helped me focus the program and stop performing 'random acts of guidance.'"

"A calendar promoted our program and kept me on schedule."

"Guidance newsletters helped to communicate our activities to staff and students."

"Our team used collective thinking to decide what data to collect and how to measure our results."

"Regularly scheduled site counselor meetings helped us to design our program."

"The district hired a guidance assistant to assist with non-school-counseling activities so we could focus on direct service to students."

Districts will find a variety of responses from the counselors, administrators, parents or guardians and teachers when the program begins its transition to become an ASCA National Model program. Collaboration and communication will provide the feedback needed to revise methods or policies hampering progression toward the goals. Regularly taking the temperature of those involved will motivate the cadre of leaders who are working to revise the program.

Expect that each school and district will adjust the implementation overview outlined above to suit local site needs. Sharing insights with neighboring or like school systems who are implementing the model will ensure the support the team needs when challenges threaten your forward progress.

Frequently Asked Questions

How does a school or district proceed to implement the ASCA School Counseling Program?

Once schools and districts adopt ASCA's National Model, a team effort is required to make the change. The team may be a counseling department, a cadre of K-12 counselors from a district or a state cadre. It is recommended that unified districts design a K-12 program even if some grades do not as yet have school counselors. The goal is to have school counselors at all levels with a ratio of 250-students-to-one-school-counselor. The process is challenging work that will take several years to complete, and the question remains, "Will it be worth everyone's time and effort?" ASCA recognizes that some schools have counseling programs facilitated by only a single counselor. As the model is not prescriptive, it can be adapted to fit a school's needs. The process may take longer, but it is equally important. Redesigning a program that has been in place for quite some time will require patience, teaming and collaborating as well. However, developing a school counseling program will bring new life into the current program and make it more responsive to the needs of students and the community.

We already have a program in place. Do we need to start over?

Absolutely not. Your team may have already developed a mission statement guiding your department's work. However, you may not have developed, discussed or presented it to your site administrator. As you will notice in the audit, collaboration and communication with administrators are important parts of the process, so you may want to do this now. Begin by taking time to reflect on the outcome of the audit, look at areas that need development or improvement and begin to move your program forward.

My team doesn't want to change; I feel alone in this.

Unfortunately, this can happen. Typically, this is often due to a fear of change. However, you can make change on you own – regardless of whether others want to change. Start by asking, "What are my students' needs?" "What do I want to accomplish?" "What do I have the power to change?" or "What am I already doing that can be measured?" From those answers, the transformation of your school counseling program can begin. By personally recognizing that something needs to be changed and allowing yourself to address that need for change, you can begin to work toward a more effective program. It can be as simple as designing, aligning and measuring the results of a single classroom guidance lesson, doing a pre-post test to see results of an

intervention program or measuring the improved attendance or behavior of a selected group of students. Once you have measured your results and shared them with others, your colleagues may want to know how they were accomplished and may begin to come on board. If not, don't be discouraged. You can still begin on your own to develop a personal action plan to align your school counseling activities to ASCA's National Standards and begin measuring the results of your guidance curriculum and interventions designed to close the gap. Sharing your action plan with your administrator early in the year will keep him or her informed as to your activities; sharing your results with your administrator, staff and colleagues may be just the push colleagues need to join you in the movement forward.

What if I have no program in place? Where do I begin?

Moving to a comprehensive school counseling program is like remodeling a house. It is suggested that counselors use the parts of the present program that fit into the ASCA National Model and then adjust or remodel the other parts over a three- to five-year time span. Two of the biggest changes are moving from a "service" to a "program" and ensuring the program measures results. The change process requires the ability to envision the future you desire for your department or district. It is not recommended to completely redesign or change everything that is being done in a school counseling department.

As you begin the journey, you will need a map. We recommend you begin by setting aside some uninterrupted time to perform a program audit. The audit contains all of the key elements in The ASCA National Model: A Framework for School Counseling Programs and provides you the opportunity to assess

Leadership is about taking "next steps." The ASCA National Model Committee members took the next steps to place the school counseling profession squarely in the education reform movement. Their work will benefit the profession for many, many years.

Mark Kuranz,
J.I. Case High School

your program's strengths, weaknesses and areas where work might begin. If you have no program in place, it may appear overwhelming in the beginning, but do not despair. During the development of ASCA's National Model, a dozen districts in California test-drove the audit. Most found they had only a few of the model components in place. However, after only three months, all had developed their mission and philosophy; all had begun to align their guidance curriculum with ASCA National Standards and had created action plans; and many were well on their way to the results of their program.

Conclusion

> **This National Model is a working document combining theory and practice. It is an essential resource for you to use in establishing or updating your school counseling program.**
>
> *Carolyn Sheldon,*
> *Lewis and Clark College*

ASCA, as well as school counseling professionals around the country, are committed to assisting districts as they create model school counseling programs. A variety of resources are available from ASCA, from school districts implementing the program and from school counselors. ASCA's next step is to develop workbooks providing hands-on materials that will assist school counselors as they implement their program.

The American School Counselor Association, as well as school counseling professionals around the country, are committed to assisting districts as they create model school counseling programs. A variety of information and materials is available from ASCA's resource center and on its Web site. In addition, check with school districts and states and with fellow school counselors, school counselor educators and school counseling graduate students. Keep current by checking the ASCA Web site for new information, and become part of the general ASCA listserv and/or one or all of the level listservs. Many questions are posted on the listservs, and wonderful answers have been shared. Many sessions at ASCA's annual conference focus on the ASCA National Model.

Keep ASCA Informed
ASCA is very interested in hearing from you. ASCA would appreciate your site and district's comments and suggestions as you engage in the change process. Please contact ASCA with your needs, struggles and successes so we may assist you and others in the collaborative effort to improve school counseling programs nationwide. ASCA truly looks forward to hearing from you soon. Contact ASCA at asca@schoolcounselor.org.

Appendix

The appendix in this document includes some examples of ways to implement the ASCA National Model. If you would like more examples of forms aligning with the model at different levels, visit ASCA's Web site, *www.schoolcounselor.org*

Evolution of The ASCA National Model: A Framework for School Counseling Programs

ASCA would not have accomplished the task of publishing the National Model without the dedicated efforts of the task force participants who met three times for seminal discussions of philosophy and content. Their continued support through the process produced The ASCA National Model: A Framework for School Counseling Programs.

JUNE 1-3, 2001, TUCSON, ARIZ.

The first ASCA National Model meeting was held June 1-3, 2001, to discuss the future of school counseling programs and to develop a framework for a national model for school counseling programs (Bowers, Hatch & Schwallie-Giddis).

Participants

Judy Bowers, ASCA supervisor/post-secondary level vice president and guidance coordinator, Tucson Unified School District, Ariz.

Trish Hatch, ASCA supervisor/post-secondary vice president-elect and coordinator of student services, Moreno Valley School District, Calif.

Pam Gabbard, ASCA president-elect and counselor at Ballard County Elementary, Barlow, Ky.

Norm Gysbers, Ph.D., University of Missouri-Columbia

Peggy Hines, Ed.D., Indiana State University, Terre Haute, Ind.

Curly (C.D.) Johnson, Ph.D., consultant, San Juan Capistrano, Calif.

Dawn Kay, Utah State Department of Education

Mark Kuranz, ASCA president and counselor at Case High School, Racine, Wis.

Stan Maliszewski, Ph.D., University of Arizona, Tucson

Pat Martin, The Education Trust, Washington, D.C.

Susan Mellegard, state guidance supervisor, Arizona Department of Education, Phoenix

Robert Myrick, Ph.D., University of Florida, Gainesville

Pat Schwallie-Giddis, Ph.D., George Washington University, Washington, D.C.

Kwok-Sze Wong, ASCA executive director, Alexandria, Va.

Criteria for Development of the National Model

Participants agreed to develop a model that would consist of three levels of program implementation: foundation, delivery and management, and evaluation. There would be four to five components in each of the three levels. The

Evolution of The ASCA National Model: A Framework for School Counseling Programs

ASCA National Standards would be the foundation upon which the program curriculum would be built.

In developing the model, participants agreed on the following assumptions and criteria:

◆ ASCA's National Standards are a framework/foundation for the development of a school counseling program. Many states also have standards aligning with ASCA's standards.

◆ A distinction must be made among the school counseling standards for every student, school counseling standards for the program and school counseling standards for the professional school counselor.

◆ A school counseling program must provide a framework allowing flexibility for states and school districts to create a program based on a district's individual needs and accountability.

◆ A school counseling program must be integral to student academic achievement, particularly in facilitating improvement in academic achievement, and must help set higher standards for student achievement.

◆ A school counseling program must be data-driven (disaggregated) and result-based and should not focus only on methods and techniques.

◆ School counseling programs should be developed and implemented districtwide, not just at individual schools.

◆ Successful development and implementation of a school counseling program relies on school/community collaboration.

◆ A school counseling program should provide intentional guidance to specifically address the needs of every student, particularly students of culturally diverse, low social-economic status and other underserved or underperforming populations.

◆ A school counseling program empowers school counselors and teaches them how to work with administrators to re-assign nonguidance activities such as master scheduling or testing.

◆ The design of a school counseling program model must include accountability tools for measuring results.

◆ To facilitate the adoption of a school counseling program model by school districts, ASCA will identify and disseminate best practices for designing, developing, coordinating, implementing, evaluating and enhancing the program.

◆ A school counseling program must include plans for the effective use of counselor time within the delivery system.

◆ A school counseling program should be preventive in design and developmental in nature.

◆ Professional school counselors play leadership roles in defining and carrying out a school counseling program.

Evolution of The ASCA National Model: A Framework for School Counseling Programs

◆ Licensed or credentialed professional school counselors must implement a school counseling program.

◆ In a school counseling program, professional school counselors work as change agents within the educational system to advocate for student needs and student results.

◆ Professional school counselors must use data to advocate for students and a school counseling program.

◆ A school counseling program should demonstrate evidence of the utilization of technology to implement the program, to advocate for the program and to collect, analyze and interpret data.

◆ In a school counseling program, school counselors strive for continued improvement and use results to continually improve the program for students.

Framework

As a basis for a National Model, participants incorporated theories and concepts from programs designed by Gysbers, Johnson, Myrick, The Education Trust, ASCA's National Standards for School Counseling Programs and others.

Meeting participants approved a preliminary model.

MAY 3-5, 2002, ALEXANDRA, VA.

The second National Model meeting was held May 3-5, 2002, to review the first draft of the ASCA National Model and to prepare for the dissemination of the model at the ASCA conference in June 2002.

Participants joining the group were:
Jill Cook, ASCA, director of programs, Alexandria, Va.
Carol Dahir, Ed.D., counselor educator, New York Institute of Technology
Reese House, Ph.D., Education Trust, Washington, D.C.
Brenda Melton, ASCA president-elect and school counselor in the San Antonio Public Schools, San Antonio, Texas
Mary Pat McCartney, Bristow Run Elementary, Bristow, Va.
Paul Meyers, consultant in the counseling and student support office, California Department of Education
Carolyn Sheldon, counselor educator, Lewis and Clark College and an ASCA past president

NOV. 8-10, 2002, CHICAGO, ILL.

The third meeting was held Nov. 8-10, 2002, to review the comments gathered during the public comment time and to look at strategies for implementation of the ASCA National Model. During the meeting, a new title, The ASCA National Model: A Framework for School Counseling Programs, was approved. In addition, consistent language was recommended regarding the use of the term *standards.*

Additional participants at this meeting were:
Russell Sabella, Ph.D., Florida Gulf Coast University, Ft. Myers, and ASCA president-elect

What is a School Counseling Program?

Reaches Every Student

Comprehensive in Scope – ASCA National Standards
(Selects measurable student competencies based on local need)
◆ Academic Domain
◆ Career Domain
◆ Personal/Social Domain

Preventative in Design

Developmental in Nature

Integral Part of the Total Educational Program

Includes a Delivery System
◆ Individual Student Planning
◆ Responsive Service
◆ System Support

Guidance Curriculum
◆ Classroom activities
◆ Interdisciplinary curriculum development
◆ Group activities
◆ Parent workshops

What is a School Counseling Program?

Individual Student Planning
◆ Individual or small-group appraisal
◆ Individual or small-group advisement

Responsive Services
◆ Consultation
◆ Individual and small-group counseling
◆ Crisis counseling
◆ Referrals
◆ Peer facilitation

System Support
◆ Professional development
◆ Consultation, collaboration and teaming
◆ Program management and operation

Implemented by a Credentialed School Counselor

Conducted in Collaboration

Monitors Student Progress

Driven by Data

Seeks Improvement

Shares Successes

ASCA National Standards for Students (Competencies and Indicators)

Legend: A:A-1.1 = Academic Domain, Standard A, Competency 1 and Indicator 1

Academic Development

Standard A: Students will acquire the attitudes, knowledge and skills that contribute to effective learning in school and across the life span.

A:A1 Improve Academic Self-concept
A:A1.1 Articulate feelings of competence and confidence as learners
A:A1.2 Display a positive interest in learning
A:A1.3 Take pride in work and achievement
A:A1.4 Accept mistakes as essential to the learning process
A:A1.5 Identify attitudes and behaviors that lead to successful learning

A:A2 Acquire Skills for Improving Learning
A:A2.1 Apply time-management and task-management skills
A:A2.2 Demonstrate how effort and persistence positively affect learning
A:A2.3 Use communications skills to know when and how to ask for help when needed
A:A2.4 Apply knowledge and learning styles to positively influence school performance

A:A3 Achieve School Success
A:A3.1 Take responsibility for their actions
A:A3.2 Demonstrate the ability to work independently, as well as the ability to work cooperatively with other students
A:A3.3 Develop a broad range of interests and abilities
A:A3.4 Demonstrate dependability, productivity and initiative
A:A3.5 Share knowledge

Standard B: Students will complete school with the academic preparation essential to choose from a wide range of substantial post-secondary options, including college.

A:B1 Improve Learning
A:B1.1 Demonstrate the motivation to achieve individual potential
A:B1.2 Learn and apply critical-thinking skills
A:B1.3 Apply the study skills necessary for academic success at each level
A:B1.4 Seek information and support from faculty, staff, family and peers
A:B1.5 Organize and apply academic information from a variety of sources

Adapted from Campbell, C. A., & Dahir, C. A. (1997). *Sharing the vision: National standards for school counseling programs.* Alexandria, VA: American School Counselor Association.

⛎ ASCA National Standards for Students (Competencies and Indicators)

A:B1.6   Use knowledge of learning styles to positively influence school performance

A:B1.7   Become a self-directed and independent learner

A:B2   **Plan to Achieve Goals**

A:B2.1   Establish challenging academic goals in elementary, middle/junior high and high school

A:B2.2   Use assessment results in educational planning

A:B2.3   Develop and implement annual plan of study to maximize academic ability and achievement

A:B2.4   Apply knowledge of aptitudes and interests to goal setting

A:B2.5   Use problem-solving and decision-making skills to assess progress toward educational goals

A:B2.6   Understand the relationship between classroom performance and success in school

A:B2.7   Identify post-secondary options consistent with interests, achievement, aptitude and abilities

STANDARD C: Students will understand the relationship of academics to the world of work and to life at home and in the community.

A:C1   **Relate School to Life Experiences**

A:C1.1   Demonstrate the ability to balance school, studies, extracurricular activities, leisure time and family life

A:C1.2   Seek co-curricular and community experiences to enhance the school experience

A:C1.3   Understand the relationship between learning and work

A:C1.4   Demonstrate an understanding of the value of lifelong learning as essential to seeking, obtaining and maintaining life goals

A:C1.5   Understand that school success is the preparation to make the transition from student to community member

A:C1.6   Understand how school success and academic achievement enhance future career and vocational opportunities

ASCA National Standards for Students (Competencies and Indicators)

Career Development

Standard A: Students will acquire the skills to investigate the world of work in relation to knowledge of self and to make informed career decisions.

C:A1 **Develop Career Awareness**

C:A1.1 Develop skills to locate, evaluate and interpret career information

C:A1.2 Learn about the variety of traditional and nontraditional occupations

C:A1.3. Develop an awareness of personal abilities, skills, interests and motivations

C:A1.4 Learn how to interact and work cooperatively in teams

C:A1.5 Learn to make decisions

C:A1.6 Learn how to set goals

C:A1.7 Understand the importance of planning

C:A1.8 Pursue and develop competency in areas of interest

C:A1.9 Develop hobbies and vocational interests

C:A1.10 Balance between work and leisure time

C:A2 **Develop Employment Readiness**

C:A2.1 Acquire employability skills such as working on a team, problem-solving and organizational skills

C:A2.2 Apply job readiness skills to seek employment opportunities

C:A2.3 Demonstrate knowledge about the changing workplace

C:A2.4 Learn about the rights and responsibilities of employers and employees

C:A2.5 Learn to respect individual uniqueness in the workplace

C:A2.6 Learn how to write a resume

C:A2.7 Develop a positive attitude toward work and learning

C:A2.8 Understand the importance of responsibility, dependability, punctuality, integrity and effort in the workplace

C:A2.9 Utilize time- and task-management skills

Standard B: Students will employ strategies to achieve future career goals with success and satisfaction.

C:B1 **Acquire Career Information**

C:B1.1 Apply decision-making skills to career planning, course selection and career transition

C:B1.2 Identify personal skills, interests and abilities and relate them to current career choice

C:B1.3 Demonstrate knowledge of the career-planning process

C:B1.4 Know the various ways in which occupations can be classified

C:B1.5 Use research and information resources to obtain career information

C:B1.6 Learn to use the Internet to access career-planning information

ASCA National Standards for Students (Competencies and Indicators)

C:B1.7 Describe traditional and nontraditional career choices and how they relate to career choice

C:B1.8 Understand how changing economic and societal needs influence employment trends and future training

C:B2   Identify Career Goals

C:B2.1 Demonstrate awareness of the education and training needed to achieve career goals

C:B2.2 Assess and modify their educational plan to support career

C:B2.3 Use employability and job readiness skills in internship, mentoring, shadowing and/or other work experience

C:B2.4 Select course work that is related to career interests

C:B2.5 Maintain a career-planning portfolio

Standard C: Students will understand the relationship between personal qualities, education, training and the world of work.

C:C1   Acquire Knowledge to Achieve Career Goals

C:C1.1 Understand the relationship between educational achievement and career success

C:C1.2 Explain how work can help to achieve personal success and satisfaction

C:C1.3 Identify personal preferences and interests influencing career choice and success

C:C1.4 Understand that the changing workplace requires lifelong learning and acquiring new skills

C:C1.5 Describe the effect of work on lifestyle

C:C1.6 Understand the importance of equity and access in career choice

C:C1.7 Understand that work is an important and satisfying means of personal expression

C:C2   Apply Skills to Achieve Career Goals

C:C2.1 Demonstrate how interests, abilities and achievement relate to achieving personal, social, educational and career goals

C:C2.2 Learn how to use conflict management skills with peers and adults

C:C2.3 Learn to work cooperatively with others as a team member

C:C2.4 Apply academic and employment readiness skills in work-based learning situations such as internships, shadowing and/or mentoring experiences

ASCA National Standards for Students (Competencies and Indicators)

Personal/Social

Standard A: Students will acquire the knowledge, attitudes and inter-personal skills to help them understand and respect self and others.

PS:A1   Acquire Self-knowledge
PS:A1.1   Develop positive attitudes toward self as a unique and worthy person
PS:A1.2   Identify values, attitudes and beliefs
PS:A1.3   Learn the goal-setting process
PS:A1.4   Understand change is a part of growth
PS:A1.5   Identify and express feelings
PS:A1.6   Distinguish between appropriate and inappropriate behavior
PS:A1.7   Recognize personal boundaries, rights and privacy needs
PS:A1.8   Understand the need for self-control and how to practice it
PS:A1.9   Demonstrate cooperative behavior in groups
PS:A1.10   Identify personal strengths and assets
PS:A1.11   Identify and discuss changing personal and social roles
PS:A1.12   Identify and recognize changing family roles

PS:A2   Acquire Interpersonal Skills
PS:A2.1   Recognize that everyone has rights and responsibilities
PS:A2.2   Respect alternative points of view
PS:A2.3   Recognize, accept, respect and appreciate individual differences
PS:A2.4   Recognize, accept and appreciate ethnic and cultural diversity
PS:A2.5   Recognize and respect differences in various family configurations
PS:A2.6   Use effective communications skills
PS:A2.7   Know that communication involves speaking, listening and nonverbal behavior
PS:A2.8   Learn how to make and keep friends

Standard B: Students will make decisions, set goals and take necessary action to achieve goals.

PS:B1   Self-knowledge Application
PS:B1.1   Use a decision-making and problem-solving model
PS:B1.2   Understand consequences of decisions and choices
PS:B1.3   Identify alternative solutions to a problem
PS:B1.4   Develop effective coping skills for dealing with problems
PS:B1.5   Demonstrate when, where and how to seek help for solving problems and making decisions
PS:B1.6   Know how to apply conflict resolution skills
PS:B1.7   Demonstrate a respect and appreciation for individual and cultural differences
PS:B1.8   Know when peer pressure is influencing a decision
PS:B1.9   Identify long- and short-term goals

ASCA National Standards for Students (Competencies and Indicators)

PS:B1.10   Identify alternative ways of achieving goals

PS:B1.11   Use persistence and perseverance in acquiring knowledge and skills

PS:B1.12   Develop an action plan to set and achieve realistic goals

Standard C: Students will understand safety and survival skills.

PS:C1   **Acquire Personal Safety Skills**

PS:C1.1   Demonstrate knowledge of personal information (i.e., telephone number, home address, emergency contact)

PS:C1.2   Learn about the relationship between rules, laws, safety and the protection of rights of the individual

PS:C1.3   Learn about the differences between appropriate and inappropriate physical contact

PS:C1.4   Demonstrate the ability to set boundaries, rights and personal privacy

PS:C1.5   Differentiate between situations requiring peer support and situations requiring adult professional help

PS:C1.6   Identify resource people in the school and community, and know how to seek their help

PS:C1.7   Apply effective problem-solving and decision-making skills to make safe and healthy choices

PS:C1.8   Learn about the emotional and physical dangers of substance use and abuse

PS:C1.9   Learn how to cope with peer pressure

PS:C1.10   Learn techniques for managing stress and conflict

PS:C1.11   Learn coping skills for managing life events

AMERICAN
SCHOOL
COUNSELOR
ASSOCIATION

ASCA National Standards for Students: Developmental Crosswalking Tool

This form is a tool that can be used to assist you in planning your overall guidance curriculum.

ACADEMIC DEVELOPMENT DOMAIN	K-2	3-5	6-8	9-12
Standard A: Students will acquire the attitudes, knowledge and skills that contribute to effective learning in school and across the life span.				
Competency A1 Improve Academic Self-concept				
A:A1.1 articulate feelings of competence and confidence as learners				
A:A1.2 display a positive interest in learning				
A:A1.3 take pride in work and achievement				
A:A1.4 accept mistakes as essential to the learning process				
A:A1.5 identify attitudes and behaviors leading to successful learning				
Competency A2 Acquire Skills for Improving Learning				
A:A2.1 apply time-management and task-management skills				
A:A2.2 demonstrate how effort and persistence positively affect learning				
A:A2.3 use communications skills to know when and how to ask for help when needed				
A:A2.4 apply knowledge and learning styles to positively influence school performance				
Competency A3 Achieve School Success				
A:A3.1 take responsibility for their actions				
A:A3.2 demonstrate the ability to work independently, as well as the ability to work cooperatively with other students				
A:A3.3 develop a broad range of interest and abilities				
A:A3.4 demonstrate dependability, productivity and initiative				
A:A3.5 share knowledge				

ASCA National Standards for Students: Developmental Crosswalking Tool

ACADEMIC DEVELOPMENT DOMAIN	K-2	3-5	6-8	9-12
Standard B: Students will complete school with the academic preparation essential to choose from a wide range of substantial post-secondary options, including college.				
Competency B1 Improve Learning				
A:B1.1 demonstrate the motivation to achieve individual potential				
A:B1.2 learn and apply critical-thinking skills				
A:B1.3 apply the study skills necessary for academic success at each level				
A:B1.4 seek information and support from faculty, staff, family and peers				
A:B1.5 organize and apply academic information from a variety of sources				
A:B1.6 use knowledge of learning styles to positively influence school performance				
A:B1.7 become a self-directed and independent learner				
Competency B2 Plan to Achieve Goals				
A:B2.1 establish challenging academic goals in elementary, middle/junior high and high school				
A:B2.2 use assessment results in educational planning				
A:B2.3 develop and implement annual plan of study to maximize academic ability and achievement				
A:B2.4 apply knowledge of aptitudes and interests to goal setting				
A:B2.5 use problem-solving and decision-making skills to assess progress toward educational goals				
A:B2.6 understand the relationship between classroom performance and success in school				
A:B2.7 identify post-secondary options consistent with interests, achievement, aptitude and abilities				
STANDARD C: Students will understand the relationship of academics to the world of work and to life at home and in the community.				
Competency C1 Relate School to Life Experience				
A:C1.1 demonstrate the ability to balance school, studies, extracurricular activities, leisure time and family life				
A:C1.2 seek co-curricular and community experiences to enhance the school experience				
A:C1.3 understand the relationship between learning and work				
A:C1.4 demonstrate an understanding of the value of lifelong learning as essential to seeking, obtaining and maintaining life goals				
A:C1.5 understand that school success is the preparation to make the transition from student to community member				
A:C1.6 understand how school success and academic achievement enhance future career and vocational opportunities				

ASCA National Standards for Students: Developmental Crosswalking Tool

CAREER DEVELOPMENT DOMAIN		K-2	3-5	6-8	9-12
STANDARD A: Students will acquire the skills to investigate the world of work in relation to knowledge of self and to make informed career decisions.					
Competency A:1 Develop Career Awareness					
C:A1.1	develop skills to locate, evaluate and interpret career information				
C:A1.2	learn about the variety of traditional and nontraditional occupations				
C:A1.3	develop an awareness of personal abilities, skills, interests and motivations				
C:A1.4	learn how to interact and work cooperatively in teams				
C:A1.5	learn to make decisions				
C:A1.6	learn how to set goals				
C:A1.7	understand the importance of planning				
C:A1.8	pursue and develop competency in areas of interest				
C:A1.9	develop hobbies and vocational interests				
C:A1.10	balance between work and leisure time				
Competency A:2 Develop Employment Readiness					
C:A2.1	acquire employability skills such as working on a team, problem-solving and organizational skills				
C:A2.2	apply job readiness skills to seek employment opportunities				
C:A2.3	demonstrate knowledge about the changing workplace				
C:A2.4	learn about the rights and responsibilities of employers and employees				
C:A2.5	learn to respect individual uniqueness in the workplace				
C:A2.6	learn how to write a resume				
C:A2.7	develop a positive attitude toward work and learning				
C:A2.8	understand the importance of responsibility, dependability, punctuality, integrity and effort in the workplace				
C:A2.9	utilize time- and task-management skills				

ASCA National Standards for Students: Developmental Crosswalking Tool

CAREER DEVELOPMENT DOMAIN		K-2	3-5	6-8	9-12
STANDARD B: Students will employ strategies to achieve future career goals with success and satisfaction.					
Competency B:1 Acquire Career Information					
C:B1.1	apply decision-making skills to career planning, course selection and career transition				
C:B1.2	identify personal skills, interests and abilities, and relate them to current career choice				
C:B1.3	demonstrate knowledge of the career-planning process				
C:B1.4	know the various ways in which occupations can be classified				
C:B1.5	use research and information resources to obtain career information				
C:B1.6	learn to use the Internet to access career-planning information				
C:B1.7	describe traditional and nontraditional career choices and how they relate to career choice				
C:B1.8	understand how changing economic and societal needs influence employment trends and future training				
Competency B:2 Identify Career Goals					
C:B2.1	demonstrate awareness of the education and training needed to achieve career goals				
C:B2.2	assess and modify their educational plan to support career				
C:B2.3	use employability and job readiness skills in internship, mentoring, shadowing and/or other work experience				
C:B2.4	select course work that is related to career interests				
C:B2.5	maintain a career-planning portfolio				
STANDARD C: Students will understand the relationship between personal qualities, education, training and the world of work.					
Competency C:1 Acquire Knowledge to Achieve Career Goals					
C:C1.1	understand the relationship between educational achievement and career success				
C:C1.2	explain how work can help to achieve personal success and satisfaction				
C:C1.3	identify personal preferences and interests influencing career choice and success				
C:C1.4	understand that the changing workplace requires lifelong learning and acquiring new skills				
C:C1.5	describe the effect of work on lifestyle				
C:C1.6	understand the importance of equity and access in career choice				
C:C1.7	understand that work is an important and satisfying means of personal expression				

ASCA National Standards for Students: Developmental Crosswalking Tool

CAREER DEVELOPMENT DOMAIN		K-2	3-5	6-8	9-12
Competency C2 Apply Skills to Achieve Career Goals					
C:C2.1	demonstrate how interests, abilities and achievement relate to achieving personal, social, educational and career goals				
C:C2.2	learn how to use conflict-management skills with peers and adults				
C:C2.3	learn to work cooperatively with others as a team member				
C:C2.4	apply academic and employment readiness skills in work-based learning situations such as internships, shadowing and/or mentoring experiences				

PERSONAL/SOCIAL DOMAIN		K-2	3-5	6-8	9-12
STANDARD A: Students will acquire the knowledge, attitudes and interpersonal skills to help them understand and respect self and others.					
Competency A1 Acquire Self-Knowledge					
PS:A1.1	develop positive attitudes toward self as a unique and worthy person				
PS:A1.2	identify values, attitudes and beliefs				
PS:A1.3	learn the goal-setting process				
PS:A1.4	understand change is a part of growth				
PS:A1.5	identify and express feelings				
PS:A1.6	distinguish between appropriate and inappropriate behavior				
PS:A1.7	recognize personal boundaries, rights and privacy needs				
PS:A1.8	understand the need for self-control and how to practice it				
PS:A1.9	demonstrate cooperative behavior in groups				
PS:A1.10	identify personal strengths and assets				
PS:A1.11	identify and discuss changing personal and social roles				
PS:A1.12	identify and recognize changing family roles				
Competency A2 Acquire Interpersonal Skills					
PS:A2.1	recognize that everyone has rights and responsibilities				
PS:A2.2	respect alternative points of view				
PS:A2.3	recognize, accept, respect and appreciate individual differences				
PS:A2.4	recognize, accept and appreciate ethnic and cultural diversity				
PS:A2.5	recognize and respect differences in various family configurations				
PS:A2.6	use effective communications skills				
PS:A2.7	know that communication involves speaking, listening and nonverbal behavior				
PS:A2.8	learn how to make and keep friends				

ASCA National Standards for Students: Developmental Crosswalking Tool

PERSONAL/SOCIAL DOMAIN		K-2	3-5	6-8	9-12
STANDARD B: Students will make decisions, set goals and take necessary action to achieve goals.					
Competency B1 Self-knowledge Application					
PS:B1.1	use a decision-making and problem-solving model				
PS:B1.2	understand consequences of decisions and choices				
PS:B1.3	identify alternative solutions to a problem				
PS:B1.4	develop effective coping skills for dealing with problems				
PS:B1.5	demonstrate when, where and how to seek help for solving problems and making decisions				
PS:B1.6	know how to apply conflict-resolution skills				
PS:B1.7	demonstrate a respect and appreciation for individual and cultural differences				
PS:B1.8	know when peer pressure is influencing a decision				
PS:B1.9	identify long- and short-term goals				
PS:B1.10	identify alternative ways of achieving goals				
PS:B1.11	use persistence and perseverance in acquiring knowledge and skills				
PS:B1.12	develop an action plan to set and achieve realistic goals				
STANDARD C: Students will understand safety and survival skills.					
Competency C1 Acquire Personal Safety Skills					
PS:C1.1	demonstrate knowledge of personal information (i.e., telephone number, home address, emergency contact)				
PS:C1.2	learn about the relationship between rules, laws, safety and the protection of rights of the individual				
PS:C1.3	learn about the differences between appropriate and inappropriate physical contact				
PS:C1.4	demonstrate the ability to set boundaries, rights and personal privacy				
PS:C1.5	differentiate between situations requiring peer support and situations requiring adult professional help				
PS:C1.6	identify resource people in the school and community, and know how to seek help				
PS:C1.7	apply effective problem-solving and decision-making skills to make safe and healthy choices				
PS:C1.8	learn about the emotional and physical dangers of substance use and abuse				
PS:C1.9	learn how to cope with peer pressure				
PS:C1.10	learn techniques for managing stress and conflict				
PS:C1.11	learn coping skills for managing life events				

ASCA National Standards for Students: Curriculum Crosswalking Tool

This form can be used to assist you in determining which standards your current or planned curriculum addresses.

	Topic of the school guidance curriculum presentation			
	Name of the specific lesson or curriculum, product or company			
ACADEMIC DEVELOPMENT DOMAIN				
Standard A: Students will acquire the attitudes, knowledge and skills that contribute to effective learning in school and across the life span.				
Competency A1 Improve Academic Self-concept				
A:A1.1	articulate feelings of competence and confidence as learners			
A:A1.2	display a positive interest in learning			
A:A1.3	take pride in work and achievement			
A:A1.4	accept mistakes as essential to the learning process			
A:A1.5	identify attitudes and behaviors that lead to successful learning			
Competency A2 Acquire Skills for Improving Learning				
A:A2.1	apply time-management and task-management skills			
A:A2.2	demonstrate how effort and persistence positively affect learning			
A:A2.3	use communications skills to know when and how to ask for help when needed			
A:A2.4	apply knowledge and learning styles to positively influence school performance			
Competency A3 Achieve School Success				
A:A3.1	take responsibility for their actions			
A:A3.2	demonstrate the ability to work independently, as well as the ability to work cooperatively with other students			
A:A3.3	develop a broad range of interests and abilities			
A:A3.4	demonstrate dependability, productivity and initiative			
A:A3.5	share knowledge			

ASCA National Standards for Students: Curriculum Crosswalking Tool

	Topic of the school guidance curriculum presentation			
	Name of the specific lesson or curriculum, product or company			
ACADEMIC DEVELOPMENT DOMAIN				
Standard B: Students will complete school with the academic preparation essential to choose from a wide range of substantial post-secondary options, including college.				
Competency B1.0 Improve Learning				
A:B1.1	demonstrate the motivation to achieve individual potential			
A:B1.2	learn and apply critical-thinking skills			
A:B1.3	apply the study skills necessary for academic success at each level			
ACADEMIC DEVELOPMENT DOMAIN				
A:B1.4	seek information and support from faculty, staff, family and peers			
A:B1.5	organize and apply academic information from a variety of sources			
A:B1.6	use knowledge of learning styles to positively influence school performance			
A:B1.7	become a self-directed and independent learner			
Competency B2 Plan to Achieve Goals				
A:B2.1	establish challenging academic goals in elementary, middle/junior high and high school			
A:B2.2	use assessment results in educational planning			
A:B2.3	develop and implement annual plan of study to maximize academic ability and achievement			
A:B2.4	apply knowledge of aptitudes and interests to goal setting			
A:B2.5	use problem-solving and decision-making skills to assess progress toward educational goals			
A:B2.6	understand the relationship between classroom performance and success in school			
A:B2.7	identify post-secondary options consistent with interests, achievement, aptitude and abilities			

ASCA National Standards for Students: Curriculum Crosswalking Tool

	Topic of the school guidance curriculum presentation			
	Name of the specific lesson or curriculum, product or company			
ACADEMIC DEVELOPMENT DOMAIN				
STANDARD C: Students will understand the relationship of academics to the world of work and to life at home and in the community.				
Competency C1 Relate School to Life Experience				
A:C1.1	demonstrate the ability to balance school, studies, extracurricular activities, leisure time and family life			
A:C1.2	seek co-curricular and community experiences to enhance the school experience			
A:C1.3	understand the relationship between learning and work			
A:C1.4	demonstrate an understanding of the value of lifelong learning as essential to seeking, obtaining and maintaining life goals			
A:C1.5	understand that school success is the preparation to make the transition from student to community member			
A:C1.6	understand how school success and academic achievement enhance future career and vocational opportunities			

ASCA National Standards for Students: Curriculum Crosswalking Tool

		Topic of the school guidance curriculum presentation			
		Name of the specific lesson or curriculum, product or company			
CAREER DEVELOPMENT DOMAIN					
STANDARD A: Students will acquire the skills to investigate the world of work in relation to knowledge of self and to make informed career decisions.					
Competency A:1 Develop Career Awareness					
C:A1.1	develop skills to locate, evaluate and interpret career information				
C:A1.2	learn about the variety of traditional and nontraditional occupations				
C:A1.3	develop an awareness of personal abilities, skills, interests and motivations				
C:A1.4	learn how to interact and work cooperatively in teams				
C:A1.5	learn to make decisions				
C:A1.6	learn how to set goals				
C:A1.7	understand the importance of planning				
C:A1.8	pursue and develop competency in areas of interest				
C:A1.9	develop hobbies and vocational interests				
C:A1.10	balance between work and leisure time				
Competency A:2 Develop Employment Readiness					
C:A2.1	acquire employability skills such as working on a team, problem-solving and organizational skills				
C:A2.2	apply job readiness skills to seek employment opportunities				
C:A2.3	demonstrate knowledge about the changing workplace				
C:A2.4	learn about the rights and responsibilities of employers and employees				
C:A2.5	learn to respect individual uniqueness in the workplace				
C:A2.6	learn how to write a resume				
C:A2.7	develop a positive attitude toward work and learning				
C:A2.8	understand the importance of responsibility, dependability, punctuality, integrity and effort in the workplace				
C:A2.9	utilize time- and task-management skills				

ASCA National Standards for Students: Curriculum Crosswalking Tool

	Topic of the school guidance curriculum presentation			
	Name of the specific lesson or curriculum, product or company			
CAREER DEVELOPMENT DOMAIN				
STANDARD B: Students will employ strategies to achieve future career goals with success and satisfaction.				
Competency B:1.0 Acquire Career Information				
C:B1.1	apply decision-making skills to career planning, course selection and career transition			
C:B1.2	identify personal skills, interests and abilities, and relate them to current career choice			
C:B1.3	demonstrate knowledge of the career-planning process			
C:B1.4	know the various ways in which occupations can be classified			
C:B1.5	use research and information resources to obtain career information			
C:B1.6	learn to use the Internet to access career-planning information			
C:B1.7	describe traditional and nontraditional career choices and how they relate to career choice			
C:B1.8	understand how changing economic and societal needs influence employment trends and future tarining			
Competency B:2.0 Identify Career Goals				
C:B2.1	demonstrate awareness of the education and training needed to achieve career goals			
C:B2.2	assess and modify their educational plan to support career			
C:B2.3	use employability and job readiness skills in internship, mentoring, shadowing and/or other work experience			
C:B2.4	select course work that is related to career interests			
C:B2.5	maintain a career-planning portfolio			

ASCA National Standards for Students: Curriculum Crosswalking Tool

	Topic of the school guidance curriculum presentation			
	Name of the specific lesson or curriculum, product or company			
CAREER DEVELOPMENT DOMAIN				
STANDARD C: Students will understand the relationship between personal qualities, education, training and the world of work.				
Competency C:1 Acquire Knowledge to Achieve Career Goals				
C:C1.1	understand the relationship between educational achievement and career success			
C:C1.2	explain how work can help to achieve personal success and satisfaction			
C:C1.3	identify personal preferences and interests influencing career choice and success			
C:C1.4	understand that the changing workplace requires lifelong learning and acquiring new skills			
C:C1.5	describe the effect of work on lifestyle			
C:C1.6	understand the importance of equity and access in career choice			
C:C1.7	understand that work is an important and satisfying means of personal expression			
Competency C2.0 Apply Skills to Achieve Career Goals				
C:C2.1	demonstrate how interests, abilities and achievement relate to achieving personal, social, educational and career goals			
C:C2.2	learn how to use conflict-management skills with peers and adults			
C:C2.3	learn to work cooperatively with others as a team member			
C:C2.4	apply academic and employment readiness skills in work-based learning situations such as internships, shadowing and/or mentoring experiences			

ASCA National Standards for Students: Curriculum Crosswalking Tool

	Topic of the school guidance curriculum presentation			
	Name of the specific lesson or curriculum, product or company			

PERSONAL/SOCIAL DOMAIN

STANDARD A: Students will acquire the knowledge, attitudes and interpersonal skills to help them understand and respect self and others.

Competency A1 Acquire Self-Knowledge

PS:A1.1	develop positive attitudes toward self as a unique and worthy person			
PS:A1.2	identify values, attitudes and beliefs			
PS:A1.3	learn the goal-setting process			
PS:A1.4	understand change is a part of growth			
PS:A1.5	identify and express feelings			
PS:A1.6	distinguish between appropriate and inappropriate behavior			
PS:A1.7	recognize personal boundaries, rights and privacy needs			
PS:A1.8	understand the need for self-control and how to practice it			
PS:A1.9	demonstrate cooperative behavior in groups			
PS:A1.10	identify personal strengths and assets			
PS:A1.11	identify and discuss changing personal and social roles			
PS:A1.12	identify and recognize changing family roles			

Competency A2 Acquire Interpersonal Skills

PS:A2.1	recognize that everyone has rights and responsibilities			
PS:A2.2	respect alternative points of view			
PS:A2.3	recognize, accept, respect and appreciate individual differences			
PS:A2.4	recognize, accept and appreciate ethnic and cultural diversity			
PS:A2.5	recognize and respect differences in various family configurations			
PS:A2.6	use effective communications skills			
PS:A2.7	know that communication involves speaking, listening and nonverbal behavior			
PS:A2.8	learn how to make and keep friends			

STANDARD B: Students will make decisions, set goals and take necessary action to achieve goals.

Competency B1 Self-knowledge Application

PS:B1.1	use a decision-making and problem-solving model			
PS:B1.2	understand consequences of decisions and choices			

ASCA National Standards for Students: Curriculum Crosswalking Tool

	Topic of the school guidance curriculum presentation		
	Name of the specific lesson or curriculum, product or company		
PERSONAL/SOCIAL DOMAIN			
PS:B1.3	identify alternative solutions to a problem			
PS:B1.4	develop effective coping skills for dealing with problems			
PS:B1.5	demonstrate when, where and how to seek help for solving problems and making decisions			
PS:B1.6	know how to apply conflict-resolution skills			
PS:B1.7	demonstrate a respect and appreciation for individual and cultural differences			
PS:B1.8	know when peer pressure is influencing a decision			
PS:B1.9	identify long- and short-term goals			
PS:B1.10	identify alternative ways of achieving goals			
PS:B1.11	use persistence and perseverance in acquiring knowledge and skills			
PS:B1.12	develop an action plan to set and achieve realistic goals			
STANDARD C: Students will understand safety and survival skills.			
Competency C1.0 Acquire Personal Safety Skills			
PS:C1.1	demonstrate knowledge of personal information (i.e., telephone number, home address, emergency contact)			
PS:C1.2	learn about the relationship between rules, laws, safety and the protection of rights of the individual			
PS:C1.3	learn about the differences between appropriate and inappropriate physical contact			
PS:C1.4	demonstrate the ability to set boundaries, rights and personal privacy			
PS:C1.5	differentiate between situations requiring peer support and situations requiring adult professional help			
PS:C1.6	identify resource people in the school and community, and know how to seek help			
PS:C1.7	apply effective problem-solving and decision-making skills to make safe and healthy choices			
PS:C1.8	learn about the emotional and physical dangers of substance use and abuse			
PS:C1.9	learn how to cope with peer pressure			
PS:C1.10	learn techniques for managing stress and conflict			
PS:C1.11	learn coping skills for managing life events			

Secondary School Counseling Program Management Agreement

(Counselor/Principal Agreement)

School Year _____ School _____ Date _____

Counselor_____

STUDENT ACCESS:
Students will access the school counselor by:

☐ a. Grade level ☐ c. Domain ☐ e. By academy/pathway

☐ b. Alpha listing ☐ d. No caseload (see any counselor) ☐ f. (Other) please specify _____

SCHOOL COUNSELOR OF THE DAY
Our counseling program will ☐ will not ☐ implement counselor of the day.

DOMAIN RESPONSIBILITIES
Looking at your site needs/strengths, counselors will be identified as the domain counselors for the following areas:

Academic domain: _____

Career domain: _____

Personal/social domain: _____

Rationale for decision: _____

PROGRAMMATIC DELIVERY
The school counseling teams will spend approximately the following time in each component area to ensure the delivery of the school counseling program?

_____% of time delivering guidance curriculum

_____% of time with individual student planning

_____% of time with responsive services

_____% of time with system support

SCHOOL COUNSELOR AVAILABILITY
The school counseling department will be open for student/parent/teacher access from _____ to _____

The department will manage the division of hours by _____

The career center will be open from _____ to _____

The department will manage the division of hours by _____

Programs and services presented and available to parents include:
Example: counseling department newsletter, parenting classes, parent information night

_____

_____

Secondary School Counseling Program Management Agreement

Programs and services presented and available to staff include:
Example: department liaison, topical information workshops (child abuse, ADD, etc.)

_____

_____

Community liaisons, programs and services will include:

_____

_____

THE SCHOOL COUNSELORS WILL BE COMPENSATED FOR EXTRA WORK HOURS (BEYOND WORK DAY) BY?

☐ Extra duty pay (fund_____)   ☐ Comp time   ☐ By principal/counselor negotiation

☐ Flex schedule   ☐ Per union regulations   ☐ No option for this

MATERIALS AND SUPPLIES
What materials and supplies are necessary for the implementation of the school counseling program?

_____

_____

The following funding resources support the school counseling program:

_____

_____

PROFESSIONAL DEVELOPMENT
The school counseling team will participate in the following professional development:

_____

_____

PROFESSIONAL COLLABORATION
The school counseling department will meet weekly/monthly:

☐ As a counseling department team   ☐ With administration

☐ With the school staff (faculty)   ☐ With subject area departments

☐ With the advisory council

OFFICE ORGANIZATION
Responsibilities for the support services provided the counseling team will be divided among the support services staff :

The school counseling assistant will: _____   The registrar will: _____

The clerk will: _____   The receptionist will: _____

Volunteers will: _____   Others will: _____

How will the agreement be monitored during the school year? _____

_____   _____
Counselor signature & date   Principal signature & date

Elementary School Counseling Management Agreement

(Counselor/Principal Agreement)

School Year _____ School _____ Date _____

Counselor_____

PROGRAMMATIC DELIVERY

The school counselor/counselors will spend approximately the following time in each component area to ensure the delivery of the school counseling program.

_____% of my time delivering guidance curriculum   _____% of my time with individual student planning

_____% of my time with responsive services   _____% of my time with system support

Lessons will be delivered in the academic, career and personal/social domain.

Programs and services presented and available to staff include:

_____

_____

Programs and services presented and available to parents include:

_____

_____

Programs and services presented and available to the community include:

_____

_____

The school counselor will be available to individual students/parents/teachers at the following times:

_____

PROFESSIONAL DEVELOPMENT

The school counselor/counselors will participate in one or more of the following professional development:

☐ Monthly district meetings for counselors   ☐ Yearly state conference

☐ Yearly national conference   ☐ Classes and/or workshops

☐ Other. Explain _____

PROFESSIONAL COLLABORATION

☐ Weekly meeting with the administration   ☐ Monthly presentation to the faculty

☐ Monthly meeting with grade level teams   ☐ Twice a year meeting with advisory council

☐ Other _____

_____   _____

Counselor signature & date   Principal signature & date

XYZ UNIFIED SCHOOL DISTRICT

XYZ Middle School Guidance Curriculum Action Plan

Year _____

Grade Level	Guidance Lesson Content	ASCA Domain/Standard	Curriculum and Materials	Projected Start/Projected End	Projected Number of Students Affected	Lesson Will Be Presented in Which Class/Subject?	Evaluation Methods How Will the Results be Measured?	Implementation Contact Person
6	Violence Prevention	Personal/Social C	"XYZ" Violence Curriculum	11/01 2/02	450	Social Studies	Pre-Post Tests Number of violent incidents	Jane Doe, school counselor
	Promotion and Retention Criteria	Academic ABC	PowerPoint District Policy	2/02 4/02	450	Language Arts	Pre-Post Tests Number of students retained	Jane Doe, school counselor
	Organizational, Study and Test-taking Skills	Academic ABC	"XYZ" Study Skills Curriculum	9/01 11/01	450	Language Arts	Pre-Post Tests Scores on Tests	Jane Doe school counselor
7	Violence Prevention	Personal/Social ABC	"Don't Laugh At Me" Ridicule Free Zones Zone	11/01 2/02	400	Science	Pre-Post Tests Number of violent incidents	Bill Jones, school counselor Mary Green, science teacher
	Promotion and Retention Criteria/ Six-Year Plan	Academic ABC	PowerPoint District Policy	2/02 4/02	400	Language Arts	Pre-Post Tests Number of students retained	Bill Jones, school counselor
	Organizational, Study and Test-taking Skills	Academic ABC	"XYZ" Study Skills Curriculum	9/01 11/01	400	Language Arts	Pre-Post Tests Scores on Tests	Jane Doe school counselor
	Organizational, Study and Test-taking Skills	Academic ABC	"XYZ" Study Skills Curriculum	2/02 4/02	400	Language Arts	Pre-Post Tests Scores on Tests	Bill Jones, school counselor, Mary Brown, language arts teacher

XYZ Middle School Guidance Curriculum Action Plan

Grade Level	Guidance Lesson Content	ASCA Domain/ Standard	Curriculum and Materials	Projected Start/ Projected End	Projected Number of Students Affected	Lesson Will Be Presented in Which Class/ Subject?	Evaluation Methods How Will the Results be Measured?	Implementation Contact Person
7	Career Exploration, (7 and/or 8)	Career AB	Career Interest Inventory	9/01 6/02	400	Exploratory	Hard copy on file of a career search Number of students who have a career path planned	Bill Jones, school counselor Each exploratory teacher
8	Violence Prevention	Personal/ Social ABC	Anti-Violence Lessons	9/01 2/02	350	Science	Pre-Post Tests Number of violent incidents	Isaac Jones, school counselor Lupe Gomez, SRO
	Promotion and Retention Criteria/ Six-Year Plan	Academic ABC	PowerPoint District Policy	2/02 5/02	350	Language Arts	Pre-Post Tests Number of students retained	Isaac Jones, school counselor
	Organizational, Study and Test taking Skills	Academic ABC	"XYZ" Testing Strategies	2/02 5/02	350	Language Arts	Pre-Post Tests Scores on Tests	Isaac Jones, school counselor
	Career Exploration (7and/or 8)	Career ABC	"XYZ" Career Interest Inventory	9/01 6/02	350	Computers	Hard copy on file of a career search Number of students who have a career path planned	Isaac Jones, computers teacher

Principal's Signature _____ Date _____ Date of staff presentation _____ Prepared by _____

XYZ SCHOOL DISTRICT

XYZ Elementary School
Closing the Gap Action Plan

Year _____

Target group: All third-, fourth- and fifth-grade students
Target group selection is based upon the following criteria: Any student who has more than 15 absences
Data that drove this decision: The systemwide attendance rate for students in grades 3-5 is 95 percent. However, at XYZ School, the attendance rate for students in grades 3-5 is 86 percent.

Counselor	Intended Effects on Academics, Behaviors or Attendance	ASCA Student Competency	ASCA Domain/ Standard	Type of Activity to be Delivered in What Manner?	Resources Needed	Projected Number of Students Impacted (Process data)	Evaluation Method How will you measure results? (Perception and results data)	Project Start/ Project End
Smith	Improved Attendance Reduction of academically at-risk students because they see that attendance affects academic progress 50 percent improvement in attendance rate within the target group from initial calculation to final calculation – 2001-2002	Apply time-management skills Use decision problem solving to foster regular attendance patterns	Academic A Personal/ Social B	Individual and/or group counseling	Funds to purchase curriculum Access to students Group counseling room	50 Students 3rd-5th Grade	Comparison of pre-post attendance records within targeted groups of students receiving individual and/or group attendance counseling Comparison of academic records Comparison of discipline records of the targeted group	11/1/2001 5/1/2002

_____ Principal's signature

_____ Date

_____ Prepared by

Attach data, examples and documentation
Submit copy to district school counselor administrator

AMERICAN SCHOOL COUNSELOR ASSOCIATION

XYZ SCHOOL DISTRICT

Guidance Curriculum Results Report

Year _____

AMERICAN
SCHOOL
COUNSELOR
ASSOCIATION

Grade Level	Guidance Lesson Content	Standards, Competencies, Indicators Addressed	Number of Guidance Lessons Delivered in What Class or Subject	Start Date End Date	PROCESS DATA (Number of students affected)	PERCEPTION DATA (Pre and post test competency attainment or student data)*	RESULTS DATA (How did the student change as a result of the lesson?)*	Implications (What do the data tell you?)

*Attach data, examples and documentation

Principal's signature _____   Date _____   Prepared by _____

XYZ SCHOOL DISTRICT

XYZ Closing the Gap Results Report

Year _____

Counselor	Target Group	Standards, Competencies, Indicators Addressed	Type of Service Delivered in What Manner?	Start Date End Date	PROCESS DATA (Number of students affected)	PERCEPTION DATA (Pre and post test competency attainment or student data)*	RESULTS DATA (How did the student change as a result of the lesson?)*	Implications (What do the data tell you?)
Berry	8th Grade: 64 students in danger of being retained at the end of Trimester 1	Standard A Competency A2 & A3 Indicator A:A2.1 & A:A3.1	Academic Counseling Groups Peer Mentoring	Sept 2002 June 2003	64	*Immediate* 99% correct on post-test knowledge of promotion information.	*Intermediate* 46 (72%) demonstrated improvement in GPA from Trimester 1 to Trimester 3. *Long term* 85% of at risk students showed improvement in GPA from Trimester 1 to Trimester 2.	Excellent academic improvement. Re-evaluate the curriculum used. Participants in the academic support groups may need further encouragement from other resources such as adult mentors.

Principal's signature _____   Date _____   Prepared by _____

*Attach data, examples and documentation

AMERICAN SCHOOL COUNSELOR ASSOCIATION

Results Reports: Impact Over Time

AMERICAN SCHOOL COUNSELOR ASSOCIATION

School _____   School Year _____   Date _____

	2000-2001	2001-2002	2002-2003	2003-2004
ACADEMIC				
Standard A – *acquire knowledge, attitude and skill leading to effective learning*				
Attendance data (ADA)				
Retention rates				
Average SAT scores				
% of minorities taking AP classes				
CAREER DEVELOPMENT				
Standard A – *acquire the skills to investigate the world of work in relation to knowledge of self and to make informed career decisions*				
% of students with interest inventories on file				
PERSONAL/SOCIAL				
Standard B – *acquire the attitudes, knowledge and interpersonal skills to help them understand and respect self and others*				
% of students suspended				
Number of conflict mediations				
NONSTANDARDS-BASED DATA				
Number of parents attending open house				
Number of volunteer mentors				

Lead counselor _____

Principal signature _____

ASCA NATIONAL MODEL : A FRAMEWORK FOR SCHOOL COUNSELING PROGRAMS

Program Audit

The program audit is used to assess the school counseling program in comparison with ASCA's National Model for School Counseling Programs. Audits serve to set the standard for the school counseling program. Audits are first performed when a school counseling program is being designed and then yearly to appraise the progress of the program development. Using the findings of both program implementation and results, strengths and weaknesses are determined, and goals are created for the following school year.

School_____Date _____

FOUNDATION

I.   BELIEFS AND PHILOSOPHY

The philosophy is a set of principles that guides the development, implementation and evaluation of the school counseling program.

CRITERIA	None	In Progress	Completed	Imple-mented	N/A
1.1 A statement of philosophy has been written for the school counseling program					
1.2 Indicates an agreed-upon belief system about the ability of every student to achieve					
1.3 Addresses every student's right to a school counseling program					
1.4 Includes a plan of closing-the-gap activities for underserved student populations					
1.5 Focuses on primary prevention, intervention and student-developmental needs					
1.6 Identifies the persons to be involved in the delivery of program activities					
1.7 Identifies who will plan and who will manage the program					
1.8 Defines how the program will be evaluated and by whom					
1.9 Includes ethical guidelines and standards					
1.10 The statement of philosophy has been presented to and accepted by administration, counselors and the advisory council					

Program Audit

II. MISSION OF SCHOOL COUNSELING PROGRAMS

The mission articulates the intentionality of the school counseling program. It represents the immediate and long-range impact (i.e., what is desired for every student five to 10 years after graduation).

CRITERIA		None	In Progress	Completed	Imple-mented	N/A
2.1	A mission statement has been written for the school counseling program					
2.2	Written with the student as the primary client					
2.3	Written for every student					
2.4	Indicates the content or competencies to be learned					
2.5	Links with the vision, purpose and mission of the state, district and the school					
2.6	Indicates the long-range results desired for all students					
2.7	The mission statement has been presented to and accepted by administration, counselors, advisory council and school board					

III. DOMAINS AND GOALS

Goals are the extension of the mission and focus on the results students will achieve by the time each student leaves the school system. The ASCA National Standards domain areas serve as the foundational goals for the school counseling program: academic, career and personal/social development. The National Standards provide a structure for the definition of goals related to competencies.

CRITERIA		None	In Progress	Completed	Imple-mented	N/A
3.1	Have been written for the school counseling program					
3.2	Reflect the domains in the ASCA National Standards for school counseling programs					
3.3	Identify a framework for organization of goals and competencies (knowledge, attitudes and skills)					
3.4	Identify the developmental structure for the school counseling program from K-12 (and beyond) and what will be measured					
3.5	Have been presented to and accepted by administration, counselors and the advisory council					

Program Audit

IV. ASCA NATIONAL STANDARDS/COMPETENCIES

Competencies are knowledge, attitudes or skills that are observable and can be transferred from a learning situation to a real-life situation and that involve the production of a measurable outcome. Competencies are indicators that a student is making progress toward the goals of the school counseling programs. They are developed and organized into content areas.

CRITERIA		None	In Progress	Completed	Implemented	N/A
4.1	Student competencies have been written that directly relate to the domains (academic, career, personal/social)					
4.2	Developmentally appropriate student competencies are specified for each grade-level grouping					
4.3	Selected competencies are based on assessment of student needs and are measurable or observable					
4.4	Goals demonstrate the link with the school counseling program mission, the school's mission and expected student results					
4.5	Written student competencies have been presented to and accepted by the administration, counselors and the school counseling advisory council					

DELIVERY SYSTEM

V. GUIDANCE CURRICULUM

Consists of structured developmental lessons designed to assist students in achieving the competencies and is presented systematically through classroom and group activities, K-12. The purpose of the guidance curriculum is to provide all students with the knowledge and skills appropriate to their developmental level. The curriculum is organized to help students acquire, develop and demonstrate competencies within the three domains: academic, career and personal/social.

CRITERIA		None	In Progress	Completed	Implemented	N/A
5.1	Guidance curriculum for all three domains has been written and adopted based on local site needs					
5.2	All students receive, in a systemic way, the content to acquire knowledge, attitudes and skills to enhance their academic, career and personal/social development					
5.3	Content is measurable (by pre-post tests, product creation or other methods)					

Program Audit

CRITERIA	None	In Progress	Completed	Imple-mented	N/A
5.4 Materials, equipment and facilities are available to support the program delivery					
5.5 Effectiveness of curriculum is evaluated annually					
5.6 The school counseling curriculum has been presented to and accepted by administration, counselors, and the school counseling advisory council					

VI. INDIVIDUAL STUDENT PLANNING

Individual student planning consists of school counselors coordinating ongoing systemic activities designed to assist the individual student in establishing personal goals and developing future plans.

CRITERIA	None	In Progress	Completed	Imple-mented	N/A
6.1 There is a systemic approach to helping students make appropriate education plans					
6.2 There is a systemic approach to helping students understand themselves through interpretation of standardized and individual tests					
6.3 A tool exists at the secondary level to assist students in making appropriate educational plans (i.e., six-year plan)					
6.4 Individual student planning includes: individual appraisal, individual advisement and appropriate student placement					
6.5 Accurate, appropriate and effective printed material is distributed to support the individual planning efforts of student and their parents					
6.6 The districtwide tools used for educational planning have been presented to the school board					

Program Audit

VII. RESPONSIVE SERVICES

Responsive services within the school counseling program consist of activities to meet the immediate need of students. These needs or concerns require counseling, consultation, referral, peer mediation or information.

CRITERIA	None	In Progress	Completed	Imple-mented	N/A
7.1 Every student K-12 receives prevention education to address life choices in academic, career and personal/social development.					
7.2 Students are assisted in solving immediate problems that interfere with their academic, career and personal/social development (i.e., conflict resolution, peer mediation)					
7.3 There is a systemic and consistent provision for the referral of students who exhibit barriers to learning					
7.4 Responsive services include: Individual and small-group counseling					
Crisis counseling					
Peer facilitation					
Consultation/collaboration					
Referral system					
7.5 A system is in place to ensure intervention for identified students.					

VIII. SYSTEM SUPPORT

System support consists of management activities that establish, maintain and enhance the total school counseling program.

CRITERIA	None	In Progress	Completed	Imple-mented	N/A
8.1 System support services have been created collaboratively with counselors and administrators					
8.2 Counselors provide professional development to staff regarding the school counseling program					
8.3 Counselors participate in professional development activities					
8.4 Counselors serve on departmental curriculum committees, district-level subject councils, community committees or advisory councils					

Program Audit

The management system is the process by which accountability for results is established and indicates who will be responsible for which students acquiring predetermined competencies.

IX. SCHOOL COUNSELOR/ADMINISTRATOR AGREEMENTS

Agreements are statements of responsibility by each counselor specifying the program results and students in which the counselor is accountable. These agreements are negotiated with and approved by the designated administrator.

CRITERIA	None	In Progress	Completed	Imple- mented	N/A
9.1 There is a clear division between assumed accountability for results and assigned duties					
9.2 The expected results are clearly delineated					
9.3 Counselors and administrators agree on assignments of counselors					
9.4 Counselors have decided how to distribute caseload and access to students – alpha assignments, domain specialization, grade level, random, counselor of the day, etc.					

X. ADVISORY COUNCIL

An advisory council is a group of persons appointed to review the program audit, goals and results reports of the school counseling program and to make recommendations to the school counseling department, principal and/or the superintendent. The membership has representation of groups affected by the school counseling program: student, parents, teachers, counselors, administrators and community.

CRITERIA	None	In Progress	Completed	Imple- mented	N/A
10.1 An advisory council has been organized and has established meeting dates and has identified tasks					
10.2 The advisory council has appropriate representative membership					
10.3 The advisory council meets at least twice a year					
10.4 The advisory panel reviews the guidance program audit, a summary of the program results reports and makes appropriate recommendations					

⚏ Program Audit

XI. USE OF DATA and STUDENT MONITORING

Analysis of data drives the program. Monitoring students' progress ensures each student acquires the identified competencies. Monitoring may be systemic by district or specific to school site, grade, class or individual, depending on site and student need. The process includes recording verification of the completion of the competency on a form (planning folder, portfolio, computer disc or other document) and measuring student improvement over time.

CRITERIA	None	In Progress	Completed	Imple-mented	N/A
11.1 District- and site-specific data on student achievement are collected and disaggregated.					
11.2 District- and site-specific data on achievement related data are collected and disaggregated.					
11.3 Standards and competency-related data are collected and disaggregated.					
11.4 Counselors are accountable for monitoring the progress of every student.					
11.5 There is an established means to monitor students' progress in guidance-related competencies, including academic achievement.					
11.6 Each student has a means to document his/her own progress, knows where documentation is kept and how to access documentation.					
11.7 Monitoring activities are determined by district, school site and grade level and are assessed over time.					

XII. USE OF DATA and CLOSING THE GAP

Analysis of data drives the program. The needs surface when program and individual data are analyzed monitoring equity and access to rigorous academic programs for every student. Monitoring of individual progress reveals interventions may be needed to support the student in achieving academic success. Data are necessary to determine: Where are we now? Where should we be? Where are we going to go? Needs are identified discrepancies between the desired results and the results currently being achieved.

CRITERIA	None	In Progress	Completed	Imple-mented	N/A
12.1 The data are disaggregated by variables such as gender, ethnicity and grade level.					
12.2 The data are systemically analyzed to determine where students are and where they ought to be.					
12.3 The identified discrepancies are aligned with the ASCA National Standards.					
12.4 The identified needs become sources for the determination of closing-the-gap activities.					

Program Audit

XIII. ACTION PLANS (GUIDANCE CURRICULUM AND CLOSING THE GAP)

For every competency taught or result anticipated by counselors, there must be a plan of how the school counselor intends to achieve the desired competency or result. Each plan contains 1) the domain, standard and competency addressed; 2) description of actual activity and curriculum used; 3) the data driving the decision to address this competency; 4) when the activity is to be completed; 5) who is responsible for delivery; 6) the means of evaluating student success – process, perception or results data; and 7) the expected result for student(s).

CRITERIA	None	In Progress	Completed	Imple-mented	N/A
13.1 Guidance curriculum action plans are drafted by the counseling team during a planning meeting					
13.2 Closing the gap action plans are drafted by the counseling team at a planning meeting					
13.3 The action plans are consistent with the program's goals and competencies					
13.4 Action plans address every aspect of the program and the academic, career and personal/social domains					
13.5 Plans include 1) the domain, standard and competency addressed; 2) description of actual activity and curriculum used; 3) curriculum or materials to be used; 4) time activity is to be completed; 5) who is responsible for delivery; 6) means of evaluating student success i.e., process or outcome data; and 7) the expected result for student(s)					
13.6 Results are stated in terms of what will be demonstrated by the student					
13.7 Every student is included in the results					
13.8 Counselors have identified specific results for which they are accountable					
13.9 Plans have been reviewed and signed by the administrator					
13.10 Action plans and closing the gap plans are completed in the spring for the next year and signed by the counselor and principal					
13.11 There are written action plans on file with the administration in charge of the school counseling program					

Program Audit

XIV. USE OF TIME/CALENDAR

A master calendar of events is developed and published to effectively plan and promote the school counseling program. To maximize active participation in the program, the calendar provides students, parents, teachers and administrators with knowledge of what is scheduled and the location and time indicating when and where activities will be held.

CRITERIA	None	In Progress	Completed	Imple-mented	N/A
14.1 The counselor's total time spent in each component of the delivery system has been compared to the ASCA National Model recommendations (see Use of Time)					
14.2 The time study is conducted and analyzed along with the program results to determine delivery system priorities					
14.3 A list of appropriate system support services (i.e., counseling/noncounseling activities) has been created					
14.4 The approved list of counseling/noncounseling activities has been approved by the board					
14.5 Master calendar exists					
14.6 The master calendar identifies grade level(s), dates and activities					
14.7 Master calendar is published and distributed to appropriate persons: students, staff, parents and community					
14.8 The counselors weekly/monthly schedule is posted					

Program Audit

ACCOUNTABILITY

XV. RESULTS REPORT

For every competency or result assumed by counselors, there must be a plan of how the school counselor intends to achieve the desired competency or result. Each results report contains 1) the domain, standard and competency addressed; 2) description of actual activity and curriculum used; 3) the data that drove the decision to address this competency; 4) when it was completed; 5) who was responsible for delivery; 6) the means used to evaluate student success – process, perception or results; and 7) the final result for student(s).

CRITERIA	None	In Progress	Completed	Imple-mented	N/A
15.1 There is an established timeline for reporting evidence of the results obtained					
15.2 Every student is included in the results					
15.3 The administrator responsible for the school counseling program has been actively involved in the negotiation of the results agreement					
15.4 A results form for the collection of results data is written and accepted by administration and school counselors					
15.5 A results form for the collection of data from closing the gap activities is accepted by the administrators and the counselors					
15.6 There is a results agreement addressing every aspect of the program and the academic, career and personal/social domains					
15.7 Process data are collected					
15.8 Perception data are collected which measures knowledge, attitudes and skills (i.e., pre-post tests; activity completed)					
15.9 Results data are collected and disaggregated measuring behaviors (i.e., graduation rates, attendance, behavior, academic achievement data over time)					
15.10 Immediate, intermediate and long-range data are collected and reviewed					
15.11 Results are reported to administrators, counselors and the school board					
15.12 Results are analyzed and used to improve the program in subsequent years					

Program Audit

XVI. COUNSELOR PERFORMANCE STANDARDS

The school counselor's performance standards used for evaluation contain basic standards of practice expected of school counselors implementing a comprehensive school counseling program. These performance standards serve as both a basis for counselor evaluation and as a means for counselor self-evaluation.

CRITERIA	None	In Progress	Completed	Imple-mented	N/A
16.1 Is written to assess the school counselor's ability to understand and implement the foundation of the comprehensive school counseling program based on ASCA National Standards					
16.2 Is written to assess the counselor's ability to implement the delivery system (i.e., guidance curriculum, individual planning with students, responsive services, system support)					
16.3 Is written to assess the counselor's ability to manage the school counseling program					
16.4 Is written to assess the school counselor's ability to measure the results of the program					
16.5 Is written to assess the counselor's use of professional communication within the school community					
16.6 Is written to determine the school counselor's fulfillment of professional growth responsibilities (i.e., use of data, technology and ethical standards)					
16.7 Is written to assess the school counselor's ability to be a leader, student advocate and systems change agent					

XVII. PROGRAM AUDIT

The program audit provides evidence of the program's alignment with the ASCA National Model. The primary purpose for collecting information is to guide future actions within the program and to improve future results for students.

CRITERIA	None	In Progress	Completed	Imple-mented	N/A
17.1 The program is audited annually					
17.2 The audit aligns with and includes all program components					
17.3 The results of the audit are shared in the spring and drive the program training and behavior for the following year					
17.4 A written long-range plan for the improvement of the school counseling program is published and revised each year					
17.5 The school counseling program has been approved by the school district's board of education					

Ethical Standards for School Counselors

Preamble

The American School Counselor Association (ASCA) is a professional organization whose members have a unique and distinctive preparation, grounded in the behavioral sciences, with training in clinical skills adapted to the school setting. The school counselor assists in the growth and development of each individual and uses his or her highly specialized skills to protect the interests of the counselee within the structure of the school system. School counselors subscribe to the following basic tenets of the counseling process from which professional responsibilities are derived:

◆ Each person has the right to respect and dignity as a human being and to counseling services without prejudice as to person, character, belief, or practice regardless of age, color, disability, ethnic group, gender, race, religion, sexual orientation, marital status, or socioeconomic status.

◆ Each person has the right to self-direction and self-development.

◆ Each person has the right of choice and the responsibility for goals reached.

◆ Each person has the right to privacy and thereby the right to expect the counselor-counselee relationship to comply with all laws, policies and ethical standards pertaining to confidentiality.

In this document, ASCA specifies the principles of ethical behavior necessary to regulate and maintain the high standards of integrity, leadership, and professionalism among its members. The Ethical Standards for School Counselors were developed to clarify the nature of ethical responsibilities held in common by school counseling professionals. The purposes of this document are to:

◆ Serve as a guide for the ethical practices of all professional school counselors regardless of level, area, population served, or membership in this professional Association;

◆ Provide benchmarks for both self-appraisal and peer evaluations regarding counselor responsibilities to counselees, parents, colleagues and professional associates, schools, and communities, as well as to one's self and the counseling profession; and

◆ Inform those served by the school counselor of acceptable counselor practices and expected professional behavior.

A.1. Responsibilities to Students

The professional school counselor:

a. Has a primary obligation to the counselee who is to be treated with respect as a unique individual.

b. Is concerned with the educational, career, emotional and behavioral needs and encourages the maximum development of each counselee.

c. Refrains from consciously encouraging the counselee's acceptance of values, lifestyles, plans, decisions, and beliefs that represent the counselor's personal orientation.

d. Is responsible for keeping informed of laws, regulations and policies relating to counselees and strives to ensure that the rights of counselees are adequately provided for and protected.

⚕ Ethical Standards for School Counselors

A.2. Confidentiality

The professional school counselor:

a. Informs the counselee of the purposes, goals, techniques and rules of procedure under which she/he may receive counseling at or before the time when the counseling relationship is entered. Disclosure notice includes confidentiality issues such as the possible necessity for consulting with other professionals, privileged communication and legal or authoritative restraints. The meaning and limits of confidentiality are clearly defined to counselees through a written and shared disclosure statement.

b. Keeps information confidential unless disclosure is required to prevent clear and imminent danger to the counselee or others or when legal requirements demand that confidential information be revealed. Counselors will consult with other professionals when in doubt as to the validity of an exception.

c. Discloses information to an identified third party who, by her or his relationship with the counselee, is at a high risk of contracting a disease that is commonly known to be communicable and fatal. Prior to disclosure, the counselor will ascertain that the counselee has not already informed the third party about his or her disease and he/she is not intending to inform the third party in the immediate future.

d. Requests of the court that disclosure not be required when the release of confidential information without a counselee's permission may lead to potential harm to the counselee.

e. Protects the confidentiality of counselee's records and releases personal data only according to prescribed laws and school policies. Student information maintained in computers is treated with the same care as traditional student records.

f. Protects the confidentiality of information received in the counseling relationship as specified by federal and state laws, written policies and applicable ethical standards. Such information is only to be revealed to others with the informed consent of the counselee, consistent with the counselor's ethical obligation. In a group setting, the counselor sets a high norm of confidentiality and stresses its importance, yet clearly states that confidentiality in group counseling cannot be guaranteed.

A.3. Counseling Plans

The professional school counselor:
works jointly with the counselee in developing integrated and effective counseling plans, consistent with both the abilities and circumstances of the counselee and counselor. Such plans will be regularly reviewed to ensure continued viability and effectiveness, respecting the counselee's freedom of choice.

A.4. Dual Relationships

The professional school counselor:
avoids dual relationships that might impair her or his objectivity and increase the risk of harm to the client (e.g., counseling one's family members, close friends, or associates). If a dual relationship is unavoidable, the counselor is responsible for taking action to eliminate or reduce the potential for harm. Such safeguards might include informed consent, consultation, supervision and documentation.

A.5. Appropriate Referrals

The professional school counselor:
makes referrals when necessary or appropriate to outside resources. Appropriate referral necessitates knowledge of available resources and making proper plans for transitions with minimal interruption of services. Counselees retain the right to discontinue the counseling relationship at any time.

Ethical Standards for School Counselors

A.6. Group Work

The professional school counselor:
screens prospective group members and maintains an awareness of participants' needs and goals in relation to the goals of the group. The counselor takes reasonable precautions to protect members from physical and psychological harm resulting from interaction within the group.

A 7. Danger to Self or Others

The professional school counselor:
informs appropriate authorities when the counselee's condition indicates a clear and imminent danger to the counselee or others. This is to be done after careful deliberation and, where possible, after consultation with other counseling professionals. The counselor informs the counselee of actions to be taken so as to minimize his or her confusion and to clarify counselee and counselor expectations.

A.8. Student Records

The professional school counselor:
maintains and secures records necessary for rendering professional services to the counselee as required by laws, regulations, institutional procedures and confidentiality guidelines.

A.9. Evaluation, Assessment and Interpretation

The professional school counselor:

a. Adheres to all professional standards regarding selecting, administering, and interpreting assessment measures. The counselor recognizes that computer-based testing programs require specific training in administration, scoring and interpretation that may differ from that required in more traditional assessments.

b. Provides explanations of the nature, purposes and results of assessment/evaluation measures in language the counselee(s) can understand.

c. Does not misuse assessment results and interpretations and takes reasonable steps to prevent others from misusing the information.

d. Uses caution when utilizing assessment techniques, making evaluations, and interpreting the performance of populations not represented in the norm group on which an instrument is standardized.

A.10. Computer Technology

The professional school counselor:

a. Promotes the benefits of appropriate computer applications and clarifies the limitations of computer technology. The counselor ensures that: (1) computer applications are appropriate for the individual needs of the counselee; (2) the counselee understands how to use the application; and (3) follow-up counseling assistance is provided. Members of under-represented groups are assured equal access to computer technologies and are assured the absence of discriminatory information and values in computer applications.

b. Counselors who communicate with counselees via internet should follow the NBCC Standards for Web Counseling.

A.11. Peer Helper Programs

The professional school counselor:
has unique responsibilities when working with peer helper programs. The school counselor is responsible for the welfare of counselees participating in peer programs under her or his direction. School counselors who function in training and supervisory capacities are referred to the preparation and supervision standards of professional counselor associations.

Ethical Standards for School Counselors

B. Responsibilities to Parents

B.1. Parent Rights and Responsibilities

The professional school counselor:

a. Respects the inherent rights and responsibilities of parents for their children and endeavors to establish, as appropriate, a collaborative relationship with parents to facilitate the counselee's maximum development.

b. Adheres to laws and local guidelines when assisting parents experiencing family difficulties that interfere with the counselee's effectiveness and welfare.

c. Is sensitive to cultural and social diversity among families and recognizes that all parents, custodial and noncustodial, are vested with certain rights and responsibilities for the welfare of their children by virtue of their role and according to law.

B.2. Parents and Confidentiality

The professional school counselor:

a. Informs parents of the counselor's role with emphasis on the confidential nature of the counseling relationship between the counselor and counselee.

b. Provides parents with accurate, comprehensive, and relevant information in an objective and caring manner, as is appropriate and consistent with ethical responsibilities to the counselee.

c. Makes reasonable efforts to honor the wishes of parents and guardians concerning information that he/she may share regarding the counselee.

C. Responsibilities to Colleagues and Professional Associates

C.1. Professional Relationships

The professional school counselor:

a. Establishes and maintains professional relationships with faculty, staff and administration to facilitate the provision of optimal counseling services. The relationship is based on the counselor's definition and description of the parameter and levels of his or her professional roles.

b. Treats colleagues with professional respect, courtesy and fairness. The qualifications, views and findings of colleagues are represented to accurately reflect the image of competent professionals.

c. Is aware of and optimally utilizes related professions and organizations to whom the counselee may be referred.

C.2. Sharing Information with Other Professionals

The professional school counselor:

a. Promotes awareness and adherence to appropriate guidelines regarding confidentiality; the distinction between public and private information; and staff consultation.

b. Provides professional personnel with accurate, objective, concise and meaningful data necessary to adequately evaluate, counsel and assist the counselee.

c. If a counselee is receiving services from another counselor or other mental health professional, the counselor, with client consent, will inform the other professional and develop clear agreements to avoid confusion and conflict for the counselee.

Ethical Standards for School Counselors

D. Responsibilities to the School and Community

D.1. Responsibilities to the School

The professional school counselor:

a. Supports and protects the educational program against any infringement not in the best interest of counselees.

b. Informs appropriate officials of conditions that may be potentially disruptive or damaging to the school's mission, personnel and property while honoring the confidentiality between the counselee and counselor.

c. Delineates and promotes the counselor's role and function in meeting the needs of those served. The counselor will notify appropriate officials of conditions which may limit or curtail her or his effectiveness in providing programs and services.

d. Accepts employment only for positions for which he/she is qualified by education, training, supervised experience, state and national professional credentials, and appropriate professional experience. Counselors recommend that administrators hire only qualified and competent individuals for professional counseling positions.

e. Assists in developing: (1) curricular and environmental conditions appropriate for the school and community; (2) educational procedures and programs to meet the counselee's developmental needs; and (3) a systematic evaluation process for comprehensive school counseling programs, services, and personnel. The counselor is guided by the findings of the evaluation data in planning programs and services.

D.2. Responsibility to the Community

The professional school counselor:
collaborates with agencies, organization and individuals in the school and community in the best interest of counselees and without regard to personal reward or remuneration.

E. Responsibilities to Self

E.1. Professional Competence

The professional school counselor:

a. Functions within the boundaries of individual professional competence and accepts responsibility for the consequences of his or her actions.

b. Monitors personal functioning and effectiveness and does not participate in any activity which may lead to inadequate professional services or harm to a client.

c. Strives through personal initiative to maintain professional competence and to keep abreast of professional information. Professional and personal growth are ongoing throughout the counselor's career.

E.2. Multicultural Skills

The professional school counselor:
understands the diverse cultural backgrounds of the counselees with whom he/she works. This includes, but is not limited to, learning how the school counselor's own cultural/ethnic/racial identity affects her or his values and beliefs about the counseling process.

ᴵ⋔ᴵᴵ Ethical Standards for School Counselors

F. Responsibilities to the Profession

F.1. Professionalism

The professional school counselor:

a. Accepts the policies and processes for handling ethical violations as a result of maintaining membership in the American School Counselor Association.

b. Conducts herself/himself in such a manner as to advance individual ethical practice and the profession.

c. Conducts appropriate research and reports findings in a manner consistent with acceptable educational and psychological research practices. When using client data for research or for statistical or program planning purposes, the counselor ensures protection of the individual counselee's identity.

d. Adheres to ethical standards of the profession, other official policy statements pertaining to counseling, and relevant statutes established by federal, state, and local governments.

e. Clearly distinguishes between statements and actions made as a private individual and those made as a representative of the school counseling profession.

f. Does not use his or her professional position to recruit or gain clients, consultees for her or his private practice, seek and receive unjustified personal gains, unfair advantage, sexual favors or unearned goods or services.

F.2. Contribution to the Profession

The professional school counselor:

a. Actively participates in local, state and national associations that foster the development and improvement of school counseling.

b. Contributes to the development of the profession through sharing skills, ideas and expertise with colleagues.

G. Maintenance of Standards

Ethical behavior among professional school counselors, Association members and nonmembers is expected at all times. When there exists serious doubt as to the ethical behavior of colleagues, or if counselors are forced to work in situations or abide by policies that do not reflect the standards as outlined in these Ethical Standards for School Counselors, the counselor is obligated to take appropriate action to rectify the condition. The following procedure may serve as a guide:

1. The counselor should consult confidentially with a professional colleague to discuss the nature of a complaint to see if she/he views the situation as an ethical violation.

2. When feasible, the counselor should directly approach the colleague whose behavior is in question to discuss the complaint and seek resolution.

3. If resolution is not forthcoming at the personal level, the counselor shall utilize the channels established within the school, school district, the state SCA and ASCA Ethics Committee.

4. If the matter still remains unresolved, referral for review and appropriate action should be made to the Ethics Committees in the following sequence:
   ◆ state school counselor association
   ◆ American School Counselor Association

☷ Ethical Standards for School Counselors

5. The ASCA Ethics Committee is responsible for educating – and consulting with – the membership regarding ethical standards. The Committee periodically reviews an recommends changes in code. The Committee will also receive and process questions to clarify the application of such standards. Questions must be submitted in writing to the ASCA Ethics

Chair. Finally, the Committee will handle complaints of alleged violations of our ethical standards. Therefore, at the national level, complaints should be submitted in writing to the ASCA Ethics Committee, c/o the Executive Director, American School Counselor Association, 101 King Street, Suite 625, Alexandria, VA 22314.

H. Resources for Ethical Standards

School counselors are responsible for being aware of, and acting in accord with, standards and positions of the counseling profession as represented in official documents such as those listed below:

American Counseling Association. (1995). *Code of ethics and standards of practice.* Alexandria, VA. (5999 Stevenson Ave., Alexandria, VA 22034) 1 800 347 6647 www.counseling.org.

American School Counselor Association. (1997). *The national standards for school counseling programs.* Alexandria, VA. (801 North Fairfax Street, Suite 310, Alexandria, VA 22314) 1 800 306 4722 www.schoolcounselor. org.

American School Counselor Association. (1998). Position Statements. Alexandria, VA.

American School Counselor Association. (1998). *Professional liability insurance program.* (Brochure). Alexandria, VA.

Arrendondo, Toperek, Brown, Jones, Locke, Sanchez, and Stadler. (1996). *Multicultural counseling competencies and standards.* Journal of Multicultural Counseling and Development . Vol. 24, No. 1. See American Counseling Association.

Arthur, G.L. and Swanson, C.D. (1993). *Confidentiality and privileged communication.* (1993). See American Counseling Association.

Association for Specialists in Group Work. (1989). *Ethical Guidelines for group counselors.* Alexandria, VA. See American Counseling Association.

Corey, G., Corey, M.S. and Callanan. (1998). *Issues and ethics in the helping professions.* Pacific Grove, CA: Brooks/Cole. (Brooks/Cole, 511 Forest Lodge Rd., Pacific Grove, CA 93950) www.thomson.com.

Crawford, R. (1994). *Avoiding counselor malpractice.* Alexandria, VA. See American Counseling Association.

Forrester-Miller, H. and Davis, T.E. (1996). *A practitioner's guide to ethical decision making.* Alexandria, VA. See American Counseling Association.

Herlihy, B. and Corey, G. (1996). *ACA ethical standards casebook.* Fifth ed. Alexandria, VA. See American Counseling Association.

Herlihy, B. and Corey, G. (1992). *Dual relationships in counseling.* Alexandria, VA. See American Counseling Association.

Huey, W.C. and Remley, T.P. (1988). *Ethical and legal issues in school counseling.* Alexandria, VA. See American School Counselor Association.

Joint Committee on Testing Practices. (1988). *Code of fair testing practices in education.* Washington, DC: American Psychological Association. (1200 17th Street, NW, Washington, DC 20036) 202 336 5500

Ethical Standards for School Counselors

Mitchell, R.W. (1991). *Documentation in counseling records*. Alexandria, VA. See American Counseling Association.

National Board for Certified Counselors. (1998). *National Board for Certified Counselors: code of ethics*. Greensboro, NC. (3 Terrace Way, Suite D, Greensboro, NC 27403-3660) 336 547 0607 www.nbcc.org.

National Board for Certified Counselors. (1997). *Standards for the ethical practice of web counseling*. Greensboro, NC.

National Peer Helpers Association. (1989). *Code of ethics for peer helping professionals*. Greenville, NC. PO Box 2684, Greenville, NC 27836. 919 522 3959. nphaorg@aol.com.

Salo, M. and Schumate, S. (1993). *Counseling minor clients*. Alexandria, VA. See American School Counselor Association.

Stevens-Smith, P. and Hughes, M. (1993). *Legal issues in marriage and family counseling*. Alexandria, VA. See American School Counselor Association.

Wheeler, N. and Bertram, B. (1994). *Legal aspects of counseling: avoiding lawsuits and legal problems*. (Videotape). Alexandria, VA. See American School Counselor Association.

Ethical Standards for School Counselors was adopted by the ASCA Delegate Assembly, March 19, 1984. The first revision was approved by the ASCA Delegate Assembly, March 27, 1992. The second revision was approved by the ASCA Governing Board on March 30, 1998 and adopted on June 25, 1998.

6/25/98

Glossary

Academic achievement: attainment of educational goals, as determined by data such as standardized achievement test scores, grades on tests, report cards, grade point averages, and state and local assessments of academic progress.

Accountability: Responsibility for one's actions, particularly for objectives, procedures and results of one's work and program; involves an explanation of what has been done. Responsibility for counselor performance, program implementation and results.

Action plan: how the counselor, or others, intend to achieve the desired result or competency; items in an action plan include: domain, standard and competency, actual activity and curriculum, time of completion of activity, data used, means of evaluation and the expected result for the student(s).

Advisory council: An advisory council is a representation of all elements of the school and community appointed to audit the school counseling program goals and to make recommendations to the department, the administration and the school board regarding program priorities.

Advocacy: Actively supporting causes, ideas or policies that promote and assist student academic, career and personal/social needs. One form of advocacy is the process of actively identifying underrepresented students and supporting them in their efforts to perform at their highest level of academic achievement.

Appraisal: evaluation instrument containing competencies, indicators and descriptors.

Articulation: A process for coordinating the linking of two or more educational systems within a community.

Assessment: a tool used to measure the criteria; includes competencies, indicators and descriptors.

Career development: the necessary skills and attitudes for successful transition from school to work or post-secondary training or education.

Closing the gap: refers to the difference in achievement levels generally between privileged students and students of color or low socio-economic status

Collaboration: a partnership where two or more individuals or organizations actively work together on a project or problem.

Competencies: define the specific knowledge, attitudes and skills students should obtain.

Comprehensive school counseling program: An integral part of the total educational program that helps every student acquire the skills, knowledge and attitudes in the areas of academic, career and personal/social development that promote academic achievement and meet developmental needs.

Consultation: a process of sharing information and ideas.

Cooperation: working in conjunction with others in a supportive way.

Counseling: a special type of helping process implemented by a professionally trained and certified person, involving a variety of techniques and strategies that help students explore academic, career and personal/social issues impeding healthy development or academic progress.

Credentialed: state certified, may include licensure. Counselors have state certification specific to the state in which they are working. Some states have reciprocity for counseling certification. Some states have licensure as well.

Crosswalk (ASCA National Standards): a matrix used in standards and curriculum alignment. The matrix lists all standards, competencies and indicators; it makes the alignment visible by showing specifically where each competency is taught developmentally by grade or within a guidance lesson.

 **Glossary**

Data-driven: decisions concerning future action that are based on information, survey reports, assessments, statistics or other forms of data.

Delivery system: the means around which the counseling program is organized and delivered; includes four components: guidance curriculum, individual student planning, responsive services and system support.

Developmental counseling program: school counseling curriculum based on the developmental age of the student and conducted on a regular and planned basis to assist students in achieving specified competencies.

Disaggregated data: data separated into component parts by specific variables such as ethnicity, gender and socioeconomic status.

Domains: broad areas of knowledge base (academic, career and personal/social) that promote and enhance the learning process.

Evaluation: a process used by an individual or group to determine progress or quality; evaluation is a key element in any improvement process.

Foundation: includes the beliefs, philosophies, mission, domains and ASCA National Standards and competencies.

Goals: the extension of the mission statement; they provide the desired student results to be achieved by the time the student leaves the school system.

Guidance curriculum: the guidance curriculum component consists of structured developmental lessons designed to assist students in achieving the competencies and is presented systematically through classroom and group activities K-12.

Inappropriate school counseling activities: any activity or duty not related to the development, implementation, or evaluation of the counseling program.

Indicator: measurable evidence that individuals have abilities, knowledge or skills for a specific competency.

Individual student planning: The individual planning component consists of school counselors coordinating ongoing systemic activities designed to assist the individual student in establishing personal goals and developing future plans.

Leadership: capacity or ability to guide others; counselors use their leadership skills in their department and in their advocacy role.

Management agreement: a statement of responsibility negotiated between the principal and counselor that includes office organization, how a program is carried out, and accountability criteria and specific results.

Management system: The management system addresses the allocation of resources to best address the goals and needs of the program. Individual staff responsibilities, accountability and the cooperation among resource persons responsible for program results are outlined.

Master calendar: A master calendar of guidance events is maintained by the school counseling staff and is distributed to teachers, students and parents on a regular basis. Planning, visibility and credibility are enhanced by effective use of a master calendar.

Mission statement: This is a statement which outlines the purpose or vision of the school counseling program. It is the long range desired outcome for students. This statement must be compatible with the stated purpose or mission of the school system within which the program operates.

Perception data: These data measure what students and others observe or perceive, knowledge gained, attitudes and beliefs held or competencies achieved.

Performance appraisal: assessment of agreed-upon goals, contributions to the school counseling program, and personal and professional characteristics. Specifies contract status recommendations and indicates summative evaluation of school counselor effectiveness.

Glossary

Performance evaluation: auditing the level of guidance and counseling program implementation and status.

Personal/social development: maximizing each student's individual growth and social maturity in the areas of personal management and social interaction.

Philosophy: A set of principles guiding the development, implementation and evaluation of the program.

Process data: method of evaluation using figures, such as numbers of students served, groups and classroom visits, to show the activities, rather than the results from the activities.

Professional school counselor: state-certified school counselor (may be credentialed or licensed depending on the state). Most school counselors have a master's degree in school counseling.

Professionalism: counselors adhere to ethical, legal and professional standards developed by state and national school counseling organizations.

Program: A coherent sequence of instruction based upon a validated set of competencies.

Program audit: assessment of the school counseling program on the components of the ASCA National Model; the primary purpose for collecting information is to guide future action within the program and to improve future results for students.

Program management: activities that develop, monitor and evaluate the implementation of the comprehensive school counseling program.

Responsive services: activities that meet students', parents' and teachers' immediate need for referral, consultation or information.

Results: demonstration of learning, performance or behavioral change after guidance and counseling program participation.

Results data: outcome data; how students are measurably different as a result of the program.

Results report: written presentation of the outcomes of counseling program activities; contains process, perception and outcome data.

Standards: the model addresses four types of standards. They are content standards, program standards, performance standards and ethical standards. Standards are statements of what should be done in each area.

Student success: a broad term for student achievement.

Systemic change: Change affecting the entire system; transformational; change affecting more than an individual or series of individuals; focus of the change is upon the dynamic of the environment, not the individual.

System support: consists of the professional development, consultation, collaboration and teaming, and program management and operation activities that establish, maintain and enhance the total school counseling program.

Use of data: the use of data to effect change within the school system is essential to ensure that all students receive the benefits of a school counseling program. School counselors know how to evaluate data from their school site.

References

Arizona Department of Education (2002). *The Arizona comprehensive competency-based guidance program handbook.* Tucson, AZ: Center for Educational Development.

Bowers, J. L. & Colonna, H. A. (2001). *Tucson Unified School District Guidance and Counseling Program Handbook.* Tucson, AZ: Tucson Unified School District.

Bowers, J., Hatch, T. .& Schwallie-Giddis, P. (2001). *The brain storm.* ASCA School Counselor, 39 (1), 16-19.

Campbell, C. A. & Dahir, C. A. (1997). *Sharing the vision: The national standards for school counseling programs.* Alexandra, VA: American School Counselor Association Press.

Connecticut School Counselor Association & The Connecticut Association for Counselor Education and Supervision (2000). *Connecticut comprehensive school counseling program.* Connecticut. Author.

Dahir, C. A., Sheldon, C. B. & Valiga, M.J. (1998). *Vision into action: Implementing the national standards for school counseling programs.* Alexandria, VA: American School Counselor Association Press.

Gysbers, N. C. & Henderson, P. (2000). *Developing and managing your school guidance program.* (3rd Ed).

Hatch, T. & Bowers, J. (2002). The block to build on. ASCA School Counselor, 39 (5), 12-19.

Hatch, T. & Holland, L.A. (2001). *Moreno valley unified district school counselor academy handbook.* Moreno Valley, CA: Moreno Valley Unified School District.

Henderson, P. & Gysbers, C. N. (1998). *Leading and managing your school guidance staff.* Alexandra, VA: American Counseling Association.

Johnson, C. D. & Johnson, S. K. (2001). *Results-based student support programs: Leadership academy workbook.* San Juan Capistrano, CA: Professional Update.

Martin, P. J. & House, R. M. (2002). *Transforming school counseling in the transforming school counseling initiative.* Washington, DC: The Education Trust.

Michigan School Counselor Association (1997). *The Michigan comprehensive guidance and counseling program.* Michigan: Author.

Missouri Department of Elementary and Secondary Education (1998). *Missouri comprehensive guidance: A model for program development and implementation.* Columbia, MO: Instructional Materials Laboratory.

Myrick, R.D. (2003). *Developmental guidance and counseling: A practical approach.* (4th ed). Minneapolis, MN: Education Media Corporation.

The Education Trust (2002). *National school counselor initiative: Met Life Foundation.* Washington, DC: Author.

The Education Trust (1997). *The national guidance and counseling reform program.* Washington, DC: Author.

Van Zandt, Z., Burke, K. H., & DeRespino, M. J. (1998). *What a school administrator needs to know about comprehensive school counseling programs.* In C. Dykman (Ed.), *Maximizing school guidance program effectiveness: A guide for school administrators & program directors* (pp. 1-7). Greensboro, NC: ERIC/CASS.

State and District Models

During the 2001 ASCA Leadership Development Institute, state presidents and president-elects were asked to send any district or state handbooks to the ASCA office to review. Thank you to the following states and districts that graciously provided materials for the authors to review. When a project of this magnitude is undertaken, it is common to discover many similarities in state and district programs. As many states are sharing materials, counselors across the country are moving closer to providing a similar school counseling program for all students. As we move forward with the vision of developing a unified framework for school counseling programs nationally, many models may contain similar information. However, it is hoped that states and districts will maintain some individuality when adapting the ASCA model.

Alaska Department of Education & Early Development. (2001). *The comprehensive counseling program for Alaska public schools: A guide for program development K-12th grade* (Rev. ed.). Juneau, AK: Author.

Arizona Department of Education (2002, 2001, 1997, 1994, 1993, 1991, 1990) *The Arizona comprehensive competency based guidance program handbook.* Tucson, AZ: Center for Educational Development

Connecticut School Counselor Association & The Connecticut Association for Counselor Education and Supervision (2000). *Connecticut comprehensive school counseling program.* Connecticut: Author.

Florida Department of Education (2001). *Florida's school counseling and guidance framework: A comprehensive student development program model.* Tallahassee, FL: Author.

Idaho Department of Education (2000). *The Idaho comprehensive school counseling program model: A guide for K-12 program development.* Boise, ID: Author.

Illinois School Counseling Association (1996). *Developmental counseling model for Illinois schools: Guidelines for program development K-12.* Illinois: Author.

Iowa School Counselor Task Force (2001). *Iowa comprehensive counseling and guidance program development guide.* Iowa: Author

Kansas (1997). *Kansas comprehensive school counseling program model and guideline.* Kansas

Lancaster Central School District (2000). *Comprehensive plan for school counselors.* Lancaster, NY: Author.

Louisiana Department of Education. *School counseling model* (1998). Louisiana: Author.

Maine School Counselor Association (1998). *Creating a shared vision for school counseling program: A framework for linking guidance curricula and program opportunities to Maine's learning results.* Maine: Author.

Marana Unified School District (1988). *Implementing a CCBG program.* Marana, AZ: Author.

Missouri Department of Elementary and Secondary Education (1998). *Guidelines for performance-based professional school counselor evaluation.* Jefferson City, MO: Author.

Moreno Valley Unified School District (2000). *Comprehensive school counseling and guidance program: The implementation year.* Moreno Valley, CA: Author.

State and District Models

National Occupational Information Coordinating Committee (1996). *National career development guidelines trainer's manual 1996.* Stillwater, OK: NOICC Training Support Center.

Nebraska Department of Education (2000). *Nebraska school counseling guide for planning and program improvement.* Lincoln, NE: Author.

New York State School Counselor Association (1993). *Providing direction, achieving potential: New York state comprehensive developmental school counseling model.* New York: Author.

North Carolina Department of Public Instruction (2001). *Comprehensive school counseling: Standard course of study K-12.* Raleigh, NC: Author.

Oklahoma State Department of Education (1996). *The school counselors' guide: Developing a comprehensive guidance program with Oklahoma standards.* Author.

Omaha Public Schools (2001). *Omaha public schools comprehensive competency-based guidance program.* Omaha, NE: Author.

Omaha Public Schools (2000). *Guide for the appraisal of counselors.* Omaha, NE: Author.

Orange County Public Schools ((1999). *Framework "99" for higher achievement: What every student should know and be able to do.* Orlando, FL: Author.

Oregon School Counselor Association (2000). *Crosswalk: Oregon common curriculum goals and the national standards for school counseling programs.* Oregon: Author.

Piscataway Township Schools (2000). *Piscataway township comprehensive developmental school counseling program, K-12.* Piscataway, NJ: Author.

Sierra Vista Unified School District (1998). *Why CCBG?* Sierra Vista, AZ: Sierra Vista Unified School District #68.

South Dakota Department of Education and Cultural Affairs (2001). *South Dakota comprehensive guidance and counseling program model (draft).* South Dakota: Author.

Sunnyside Unified School District Couneling Task Force (1999). *Comprehensive competency based guidance plan.* Tucson, AZ: Sunnyside Unified School District.

Tennessee Department of Education. *Framework for evaluation and professional growth.* Tennessee: Author.

Texas Education Agency (1998). *A model developmental guidance and counseling program for Texas public schools: A guide for program development pre-K-12th grade.* Austin, TX: Author.

The National Consortium of State Guidance Leaders (2000). *A state guidance leadership implementation and resource guide.* Columbus, OH: Center on Education and Training for Employment.

Tucson Unified School District (1993, 1995, 1998, 2000, 2002). *Guidance and counseling program handbook K-12.* Tucson, AZ: Tucson Unified School District.

Utah State Office of Education (1998). *Model for Utah comprehensive counseling and guidance programs.* Salt Lake City, UT: Author.

Wisconsin Department of Public Instruction (1997). *The Wisconsin developmental guidance model: A resource and planning guide.* Milwaukee, WI: Author.

Suggested Reading

Bemak, F. (1998). Interdisciplinary collaboration for social change: Redefining the counseling profession. In C. C. Lee & G. R. Walt (Eds.), *Social action: A mandate for counselors* (pp. 279–292). Alexandria, VA: American Counseling Association.

Bemak, F. (2000). Transforming the role of the counselor to provide leadership in educational reform through collaboration. *Professional School Counseling, 3,* 323–331.

Bloom, J. (1994). *Impact research: The effects of comprehensive competency based guidance programs in Arizona schools.* Arizona Counseling Journal, 19, 27-39.

Bloom, J. (1996). *Student, administrator, counselor, and teacher CCBG successes in Arizona schools.* ERIC Digest, EDO_CB-96-20.

Borders, L. D., & Drury, S. M. (1992). Comprehensive school counseling programs: A review for policymakers and practitioners. *Journal of Counseling and Development, 70,* 487–498.

Brown, D. (1999). *Improving academic achievement: What school counselors can do?* Greensboro, NC: ERIC Clearinghouse on Counseling and Student Services (ERIC Digest ED 435895).

Burnham, J. J., & Jackson, C. M. (2000). School counselor roles: Discrepancies between actual practice and existing models. *Professional School Counseling, 4,* 41–49.

Clark, M., & Stone, C. (2000). The developmental school counselor as educational leader. In J. Wittmer (Ed.), *Managing your school counseling program: K–12 developmental strategies* (2nd ed., pp. 75–81). Minneapolis, MN: Educational Media.

Erford, B. T., House, R. M., & Martin, P. J. (2003). Transforming the school counseling profession. In B. T. Erford (Ed.), *Transforming the school counseling profession* (pp. 1–20). Upper Saddle River, NJ: Merrill Prentice-Hall.

Green, A., & Keys, S. (2001). Expanding the developmental school counseling paradigm: Meeting the needs of the 21st century student. *Professional School Counseling, 5,* 84–95.

Gysbers, N. C. (2001). School guidance and counseling in the 21st century: Remember the past into the future. *Professional School Counseling, 5,* 96–105.

Gysbers, N. C., & Henderson, P. (2001). Comprehensive guidance and counseling programs: A rich history and a bright future. *Professional School Counseling, 4,* 246–256.

Gysbers, N. C., & Henderson, P. (2002). *Implementing comprehensive school guidance programs: Critical leadership issues and successful responses.* Greensboro, NC: CAPS

Harrison, T. C. (2000). The school counselor as consultant/coordinator. In J. Wittmer, *Managing your school counseling program, K–12 developmental strategies* (2nd ed., pp.183–191).Minneapolis, MN: Educational Media.

Hart, P. J., & Jacobi, M. (1992). *From gatekeeper to advocate: Transforming the role of the school counselor.* New York: College Entrance Examination Board.

Herr, E. L. (2001). The impact of national policies, economics, and school reform on comprehensive guidance programs. *Professional School Counseling, 4,* 236–245.

House, R. M., & Hayes, R. L. (2002). School counselors: Becoming key players in school reform. *Professional School Counseling, 5,* 249–256.

ili Suggested Reading

House, R. M., & Martin, P. J. (1998). Advocating for better futures for all students: A new vision for school counselors. *Education, 119,* 284–291.

Hughes, D. K., & James, S. H. (2001). Using accountability to protect a school counseling program. *Professional School Counseling, 4,* 306–310.

Johnson, C. D., & Johnson, S. K. (1982). Competency-based training of career development specialists or "let's get off the calf path." *Vocational Guidance Quarterly, 32,* 327–335.

Johnson, R. S. (1996). *Setting our sights: Measuring equity in school change.* The Achievement Council. Los Angeles, CA.

Johnson, S., & Ammon, T. (1994). *The Arizona experience: A statewide approach to implementing competency based guidance programs for all students.* Arizona Counseling Journal, 19, 45-51.

Johnson, S. & Whitfield, E. (Eds.). (1991). *Evaluating guidance and programs: A practitioner's guide.* Iowa; American College Testing Company.

Johnson, S. K. & Johnson, C.D., (1991). *The New Guidance: A systems approach to pupil personnel programs.* A California School Counselor's Convention presentation paper, April 1991.

Kaplan, L. S. (1999). Hiring the best school counseling candidates to promote students' achievement. *NASSP Bulletin, 83,* 34–39.

Kaplan, L. (2000). Maximizing school counselors' effect on student achievement. *The High School Magazine,* pp. 5–8.

Keys, S. G., & Lockhart, E. (2000). The school counselor's role in facilitating multisystemic change. *Professional School Counseling, 3,* 101–107.

Lapan, R. T. (2001). Results-based comprehensive guidance and counseling programs: A framework for planning and evaluation. *Professional School Counseling, 4,* 289.

Lapan, R. T., Gysbers, N. C., & Petroski, G. F. (2001). Helping seventh graders be safe and successful: A statewide study of the impact of comprehensive guidance and counseling programs. *Journal of Counseling and Development, 79,* 320–330.

Lapan, R. T., Gysbers, N. C., & Sun, Y. (1997). The impact of more fully implemented guidance programs on the school experiences of high school students: A statewide evaluation study. *Journal of Counseling and Development, 75,* 292–302.

Lenhardt, A. C., & Young, P. A. (2001). Proactive strategies for advancing elementary school counseling programs: A blueprint for the new millennium. *Professional School Counseling, 4,* 187–195.

MacDonald, G., & Sink, C. A. (1999). A qualitative developmental analysis of comprehensive guidance programs in schools in the United States. *British Journal of Guidance and Counselling, 27,* 415–430.

Mau, W. C., Hitchcock, R., & Calvert, C. (1998). High school students' career plans: The influence of others' expectations. *Professional School Counseling, 2,* 161–166.

Mullis, F., & Otwell, P. (1997). Counselor accountability: A study of counselor effects on academic achievement and student behaviors. *Georgia School Counselors Association Journal, 1*(4), 4–12.

Myrick, R. D. (2002). Peer mediation and conflict resolution. In. S. E. Brock, P. J. Lazarus, & S. R. Jimerson (Eds.), *Best practices in school crisis prevention and intervention.* Bethesda, MD: National Association of School Psychologists.

Suggested Reading

Myrick, R. D. (1990). Retrospective measurement: An accountability tool. *Elementary School Guidance and Counseling. 25*(1), 21–29.

Napierkowski, C. M., & Parsons, R. D. (1995). Diffusion of innovation: Implementing changes in school counselor roles and functions. *The School Counselor, 42*, 364–369.

Paisley, P. O. (2001). Maintaining and enhancing the developmental focus in school counseling programs. *Professional School Counseling, 4*, 271–277.

Paisley, P. O., & Borders, L. D. (1995). School counseling: An evolving specialty. *Journal of Counseling and Development, 74*, 150–153.

Paisley, P. O., & DeAngelis, S. (1995). Developmental principles: A framework for school counseling programs. *Elementary School Guidance and Counseling, 30*, 85–93.

Paisley, P. O., & Hayes, R. L. (2000). Counselor under construction: Implications for constructivist-developmental program design. In G. McAuliffe, K. Eriksen, & Associates (Eds.), *Preparing counselors and therapists: Creating constructivist and developmental programs* (pp. 77–98). Alexandria, VA: Association for Counselor Education and Supervision.

Paisley, P. O., & McMahon, G. (2001). School counseling for the 21st century: Challenges and opportunities. *Professional School Counseling, 5*, 106–115.

Perusse, R., Goodnough, G. E., & Noel, C. J. (2001). Use of the national standards for school counseling programs in preparing school counselors. *Professional School Counseling, 5*, 49–56.

Reynolds, S. E., & Hines, P. L. (2001). *Guiding all kids: Systemic guidance for achievement focused schools* (2nd ed.). Bloomington, IN: American Student Achievement Institute. Retrievable at http://asai.indstate.edu

Reynolds, S. E., & Hines, P. L. (2001). *Vision-to-action: A step-by-step activity guide for systemic educational reform* (6th ed.). Bloomington, IN: American Student Achievement Institute. Retrievable at http://asai.indstate.edu

Sears, S. J. (1999, January). Transforming school counseling: Making a difference for students. *NASSP Bulletin*, pp. 47–53.

Sink, C. A., & MacDonald, G. (1998). The status of comprehensive guidance and counseling in the United States. *Professional School Counseling, 2*, 88–94.

Sink, C. A., & Yillik-Downer, A. (2001). School counselors' perceptions of comprehensive guidance and counseling programs: A national survey. *Professional School Counseling, 4*, 278–288.

Schmidt, J. J. (1999). Counseling in schools: *Essential services and comprehensive programs* (3rd ed.). Boston: Allyn & Bacon.

Schmidt, J. J., Lanier, S., & Cope, L. (1999). Elementary school guidance and counseling: The last 20 years. *Professional School Counseling, 2*, 250–257.

The Education Trust, (2002). *Achievement in America: 2001* [Computer diskette]. Washington, DC: Author [Producer and Distributor].

The Education Trust, (1999). Ticket to nowhere: The gap between leaving high school and entering college and high-performing jobs. *Thinking K–16, 3*(2), 1–32

VanZandt, Z., & Hayslip, J. (2001). *Developing your school counseling program.* Stamford, CT: Wadsworth.

Watkins, C. (2001). Comprehensive guidance programs in an international context. *Professional School Counseling, 4*, 262–270.

Suggested Reading

Watts, V., & Thomas, B. (1997). Proving that counseling programs do count: The counseling accountability. *Georgia School Counselors Association Journal, 1*(4), 1-3.

Whiston, S. C., & Sexton, T. L. (1998). A review of school counseling outcome research: Implications for practice. *Journal of Counseling and Development, 76,* 412–426.

Whiston, S. C., Sexton, T. L., & Lasoff, D. L. (1998). Career-intervention outcome: A replication and extension of Oliver and Spokane 1988. *Journal of Counseling Psychology, 45,* 150–165.

Wittmer, J. (2000). *Managing your school counseling program: K–12 developmental strategies* (2nd ed.). Minneapolis, MN: Educational Media.

Recognized ASCA Model Program (RAMP)

Drive your school counseling program to the next level. Show your administrators, school board and the community at large that you're committed to delivering a comprehensive, data-driven school counseling program. Apply for the Recognized ASCA Model Program (RAMP) designation from the American School Counselor Association.

Based on the ASCA National Model: A Framework for School Counseling Programs, the RAMP designation:
- Gives you the confidence that your program aligns with a nationally accepted and recognized model
- Helps you evaluate your program and identify areas for improvement
- Increases your skills and knowledge of school counseling
- Enhances your program's efforts toward academic achievement and student success
- Identifies your school as an exemplary educational environment

RAMP applications are reviewed three times a year. Submission deadlines are Jan. 1, March 1 and Oct. 1. To apply, complete the following application. For more information about the many benefits of achieving RAMP status, visit *www.schoolcounselor.org* and click on "National Model and RAMP."

Recognized ASCA Model Program Application

Congratulations on your decision to RAMP up your school counseling program. The following instructions will guide you through the RAMP application process.

Also included in this packet are:
- the scoring rubric to help you see what the judges will be looking for when evaluating your application.

Please use each component page as a cover page, placing your answers and documentation immediately behind the cover page. Once you've completed all 12 sections, put it in a binder, include a copy of the demographic/payment information form along with your application fee of $150 and send to: ASCA RAMP Application, 1101 King St., Suite 625, Alexandria, VA 22314.

Application deadlines are three times a year: Oct. 1, Jan. 1 and March 1. RAMP status will be awarded to schools with scores of 42 or higher, provided none of the sections receive an average score of "minimal' (2) or "unsatisfactory (1). Scoring criteria are included on each component page.

By submitting your application, you are giving ASCA permission to share and reproduce your materials with appropriate citation given to your school. All documentation must be from the current academic year or last year. Documentation more than a year old will not be accepted.

You must submit FOUR complete binders.

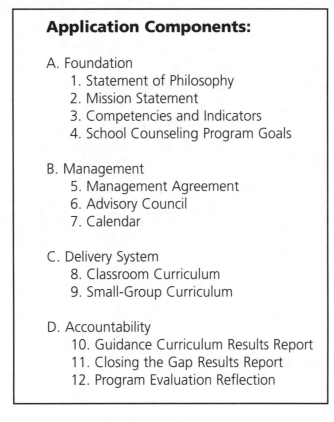

Application Components:

A. Foundation
    1. Statement of Philosophy
    2. Mission Statement
    3. Competencies and Indicators
    4. School Counseling Program Goals

B. Management
    5. Management Agreement
    6. Advisory Council
    7. Calendar

C. Delivery System
    8. Classroom Curriculum
    9. Small-Group Curriculum

D. Accountability
    10. Guidance Curriculum Results Report
    11. Closing the Gap Results Report
    12. Program Evaluation Reflection

AMERICAN
SCHOOL
COUNSELOR
ASSOCIATION

Applicant Information

Contact Name _____

Title _____

School _____

Address _____

City _____ State _____ ZIP code _____

Phone _____ Fax _____ E-mail _____

Payment Information

_____ Application fee ($150 per application)

_____ Purchase order handling charge, $10

_____ Total

☐ Check
☐ Purchase Order
☐ Credit card   ☐ American Express   ☐ VISA   ☐ Mastercard

Credit Card No. _____ Exp. Date _____

Signature _____

School Demographic Information

Grade levels served at school _____

Number of students at school _____ Number of students in district _____

Number of staff at school _____ Number of school counselors at school _____

Average number of students served by each counselor_____

School setting is:
    ☐ Urban   ☐ Rural   ☐ Suburban

Number of students identified as special education students _____

How many students receiver free lunch _____ reduced lunch _____

Ethnicity/Percentage of students who are:
_____ Black
_____ Asian
_____ Native American
_____ White
_____ Hispanic
_____ Other

A. FOUNDATION
1. Statement of Philosophy

Attach a copy of your school counseling program philosophy statement. Include signatures from the following stakeholders to verify the statement was presented and accepted: school principal, all school counselors at the school, advisory council representatives and school board representative. See the next page for an example.

Statement of Philosophy Scoring Rubric

4	**3**	**2**	**1**
Exemplary statement of philosophy that includes an agreed-upon belief system about the ability of every student to achieve and includes ethical guidelines and standards. There is evidence that the statement of philosophy has been presented to and accepted by the school's administration, counselors, the advisory council and school board.	Adequate statement of philosophy that includes an agreed-upon belief system about the ability of every student to achieve and includes ethical guidelines and standards. There is adequate evidence that the statement of philosophy has been presented to and accepted by the school's administration, counselors, the advisory council and school board.	Partial statement of philosophy that includes an agreed-upon belief system about the ability of every student to achieve and/or includes ethical guidelines and standards. There is some evidence the statement of philosophy has been presented to and accepted by either the school's administration or counselors or advisory council.	Weak or no statement of philosophy for the school's counseling program. No documentation that the philosophy statement has been presented to and accepted by the school's administration, counselors or advisory council.

Example: Sample Philosophical Statement

The counselors in XYZ school believe:
- *All students have dignity and worth*
- *All students have the right to participate in the school counseling program*
- *All students' ethnic, cultural, racial, sexual differences and special needs are considered in planning and implementing the school counseling program*
- *All students K-12 shall have access to a full-time, state-certified, master's-degree-level school counselor to deliver the counseling program*

And that the XYZ comprehensive school counseling program should:
- *Be based on specified goals and developmental student competencies for all students K-12*
- *Be planned and coordinated by school counseling teams in coordination with other school, parent or guardian and community representatives*
- *Utilize the many combined resources of the community to deliver programs*
- *Use data to drive program development and evaluation*
- *Be evaluated by a counseling supervisor on specified goals and agreed upon student competencies*
- *Actively involve counseling team members to monitor students' results*

And that all counselors in the XYZ school:
- *Abide by the professional school counseling ethics as advocated by the American School Counselor Association*
- *Participate in professional development activities essential to maintain a quality school counseling program*

Accepted by:

Principal: ─────────────────────────────

School counselor: ─────────────────────────────

School counselor: ─────────────────────────────

School counselor: ─────────────────────────────

Advisory council: ─────────────────────────────

Advisory council: ─────────────────────────────

Advisory council: ─────────────────────────────

School board representative: ─────────────────────────────

2. Mission Statement

Attach copies of your school counseling mission statement and the school's mission statement. The school counseling mission statement must be tied to the school's mission statement and must be presented to and accepted by the administration, counselors, advisory council and school board. See the example on the next page.

Mission Statement Scoring Rubric			
4	**3**	**2**	**1**
Strong mission statement that links with the vision and purpose of the school's mission statement. There is ample evidence that the mission statement has been presented to and accepted by the school's administration, counselors and school board. Indicates the general content of the program and defines the school counselor's role in helping the school manifest its mission.	Satisfactory mission statement that reasonably links to the vision and purpose of the school's mission statement. There is evidence that the statement has been presented to and accepted by the school's administration, counselors, advisory council and the school board.	Weak mission statement that tries to link to the vision and purpose of the school's mission statement. Some indication the mission statement has been presented to and accepted by the school's administration, counselors, advisory council and school board	Minimal or no mission statement or a mission statement that doesn't link to the vision and purpose of the school's mission statement. No documentation that the mission statement has been presented to and accepted by the school's administration, counselors advisory council or school board.

Example: Sample Mission Statements

XYZ School District
The mission of XYZ Unified School District is to prepare all students academically and socially to contribute at the highest levels as productive members of society, through a partnership of empowered students, educators, parents or guardians and the community responsible for the learning process.

School Counseling Program Mission Statement
The mission of XYZ Unified School District school counseling program is to provide a comprehensive, developmental counseling program addressing the academic career and personal/social development of all students. School counselors are professional school advocates who provide support to maximize student potential and academic achievement. In partnership with other educators, parents or guardians and the community, school counselors facilitate the support system to ensure all students in XYZ School District have access to and are prepared with the knowledge and skills to contribute at the highest level as productive members of society.

Accepted by:

Principal: ——————————————————————————

School counselor: ——————————————————————

School counselor: ——————————————————————

School counselor: ——————————————————————

Advisory council: ———————————————————————

Advisory council: ———————————————————————

Advisory council: ———————————————————————

School board representative: ————————————————

3. Competencies and Indicators

Fill out the template on the following page, or use one of your own.

Competencies and Indicators Scoring Rubric			
4	**3**	**2**	**1**
Developmentally appropriate and measurable competencies and/or indicators are identified for each applicable grade level and directly link to the counseling program's mission. Each competency and/or indicator appropriately relates to its ASCA standard. All ASCA standards are adequately covered across grade levels. There is evidence the standards and competencies have been presented to and accepted by the school's administration, counselors and advisory council.	Developmentally appropriate competencies and/or indicators are identified for each applicable grade level and link to the counseling program's mission. Each competency and/or indicator appropriately relates to its ASCA standard. All ASCA standards are adequately covered across grade levels. There is indication the standards and competencies have been presented to and accepted by the school's administration, counselors and advisory council.	Some competencies and/or indicators are identified for each applicable grade level but do not clearly link to the counseling program's mission. There is some indication that the standards and competencies have been presented to and accepted by the school's administration, counselors and advisory council.	Few or no competencies and/or indicators are identified and those identified do not clearly link to the counseling program's mission. There is little or no evidence the standards and competencies have been presented to and accepted by the school's administration, counselors and advisory council.

Template: Standards, Competencies and Indicators

Complete this form by entering the competencies and/or indicators that your school has approved under each ASCA National Standard.

ACADEMIC DEVELOPMENT DOMAIN	Grade Levels:						
Standard A: Students will acquire the attitudes, knowledge and skills that contribute to effective learning in school and across the life span.							

ACADEMIC DEVELOPMENT DOMAIN	Grade Levels:						
Standard B: Students will complete school with the academic preparation essential to choose from a wide range of substantial post-secondary options, including college.							

ACADEMIC DEVELOPMENT DOMAIN

STANDARD C: Students will understand the relationship of academics to the world of work and to life at home and in the community.

CAREER DEVELOPMENT DOMAIN   **Grade Levels:**

STANDARD A: Students will acquire the skills to investigate the world of work in relation to knowledge of self and to make informed career decisions.

CAREER DEVELOPMENT DOMAIN   **Grade Levels:**

STANDARD B: Students will employ strategies to achieve future career goals with success and satisfaction.

CAREER DEVELOPMENT DOMAIN Grade Levels:

STANDARD C: Students will understand the relationship between personal qualities, education, training and the world of work.

PERSONAL/SOCIAL DOMAIN Grade Levels:

STANDARD A: Students will acquire the knowledge, attitudes and interpersonal skills to help them understand and respect self and others.

PERSONAL/SOCIAL DOMAIN   **Grade Levels:**

STANDARD B: Students will make decisions, set goals and take necessary action to achieve goals.

PERSONAL/SOCIAL DOMAIN   **Grade Levels:**

STANDARD C: Students will understand safety and survival skills.
Competency C1 Acquire Personal Safety Skills

Principal: _____

School counselor: _____   *School counselor:* _____

School counselor: _____   *Advisory council:* _____

Advisory council: _____   *Advisory council:* _____

School board representative: _____

RAMP Application

4. School Counseling Program Goals

Attach copies of your school counseling program goals for the current or previous academic year as well as information on how you selected these goals. Include documentation or any data you used to arrive at these goals.

Example: School Counseling Program Goals

A. *By the end of the school year, attendance will improve by 10 percent.*

B. *By the end of the school year, the number of office referrals for bullying will decrease by 25 percent over last year.*

C. *School counselors will spend 60 percent of their time in direct service to students.*

Principal: _____

School counselor: _____

School counselor: _____

School counselor: _____

Advisory council: _____

Advisory council: _____

Advisory council: _____

School Counseling Program Goals Scoring Rubric

4	3	2	1
Exemplary school counseling program goals reflecting prioritized ASCA National Standards. There is evidence the program's goals are based upon school data and reflect the domains of the ASCA National Standards. There is evidence the goals have been presented to and accepted by the school's administration, counselors and the advisory council.	Adequate school counseling program goals reflecting prioritized ASCA National Standards. There is evidence the goals have been presented to and accepted by the school's administration, counselors and the advisory council.	Incomplete school counseling program goals that somewhat reflect the domains of the ASCA National Standards for School Counseling Programs. There is some evidence the goals have been presented to and accepted by the school's administration, counselors and the advisory council.	Inadequate or no school counseling program goals that don't reflect the domains of the ASCA National Standards for School Counseling Programs. There is little or no evidence the goals have been presented to and accepted by the school's administration, counselors and the advisory council.

B. MANAGEMENT

5. Management Agreement

Attach a copy of the management agreement for each counselor in the school. Be sure the agreement includes the percentage of time allocated for each delivery area. You can use one of the sample agreements provided, or you can use one of your own.

Management Agreement Scoring Rubric

4	3	2	1
Comprehensive and thorough management agreement for each counselor at the school is included. The percentage of time spent in each delivery area reflects the school counseling program goals. Each agreement is signed by the school counselor and the school's principal. Each agreement reflects the school counseling program mission statement and goals.	A management agreement for each counselor at the school is included, showing the percentage of time spent in each delivery area. Each agreement is signed by the school counselor and the school's principal. Each agreement reflects the school counseling program mission statement and goals.	A weak management agreement for each counselor at the school is evident; it does not show the percentage of time spent in each delivery area. Each agreement may be signed by the school counselor and the school's principal.	No management agreement for counselors at the school is evident.

Example: Elementary School Counselor Management Agreement

School Year _____ School_____ Date _____

Counselor_____

PROGRAMMATIC DELIVERY

The school counselor/counselors will spend approximately the following time in each component area to ensure the delivery of the school counseling program.

_____% of time delivering guidance curriculum _____% of time with individual student planning

_____% of time with responsive services _____% of time with system support

Lessons will be delivered in the academic, career and personal/social domain.

Programs and services presented and available to staff include:

_____

_____

Programs and services presented and available to parents include:

_____

_____

Programs and services presented and available to the community include:

_____

_____

The school counselor will be available to individual students/parents/teachers at the following times:

_____

PROFESSIONAL DEVELOPMENT

The school counselor/counselors will participate in one or more of the following professional development:

☐ Once a month district meetings for counselors ☐ Yearly state conference

☐ Yearly national conference ☐ Classes and/or workshops Other. Explain _____

PROFESSIONAL COLLABORATION

☐ Once a week meeting with the administration ☐ Once a month present something to the faculty

☐ Once a month meeting with grade level teams ☐ Twice a year meeting with advisory council

Other _____

How will this agreement be monitored during the school year? _____

_____   _____

Counselor signature & date   Principal signature & date

AMERICAN
SCHOOL
COUNSELOR
ASSOCIATION

Secondary School Counseling Program Management Agreemen

(Counselor/Principal Agreement)

School Year _____ School _____ Date _____

Counselor_____

STUDENT ACCESS:
Students will access the school counselor by:

☐ a. Grade level   ☐ c. Domain   ☐ e. By academy/pathway

☐ b. Alpha listing   ☐ d. No caseload (See any counselor)   ☐ F. (Other) please specify _____

SCHOOL COUNSELOR OF THE DAY
Our counseling program will ☐ will not ☐ implement counselor of the day.

DOMAIN RESPONSIBILITIES
Looking at your site needs/strengths, counselors will be identified as the domain counselors for the following areas:

Academic domain: _____

Career domain: _____

Personal/social domain: _____

Rationale for decision: _____

PROGRAMMATIC DELIVERY
The school counseling teams will spend approximately the following time in each component area to ensure the delivery of the school counseling program?

_____% of time delivering guidance curriculum

_____% of time with individual student planning

_____% of time with responsive services

_____% of time with system support

SCHOOL COUNSELOR AVAILIBILITY
The school counseling department be open for student/parent/teacher access from _____ to _____

The department will manage the division of hours by: _____

The career center will be open from _____ to _____

The department will manage the division of hours by: _____

Programs and services presented and available to parents include:
Example: counseling department newsletter, parenting classes, parent information night

_____

_____

Secondary School Counseling Program Management Agreement

Programs and services presented and available to staff include:
Example: department liaison, topical information workshops (child abuse, ADD, etc.)

_____

_____

Community liaisons, programs and services will include:

_____

_____

THE SCHOOL COUNSELORS WILL BE COMPENSATED FOR EXTRA WORK HOURS (BEYOND WORK DAY) BY?

☐ Extra duty pay (fund?) ☐ Comp time ☐ By principal/counselor negotiation

☐ Flex schedule ☐ Per union regulations ☐ No option for this

MATERIALS AND SUPPLIES
What materials and supplies are necessary for the implementation of the school counseling program:

_____

_____

The following funding resources support the school counseling program:

_____

_____

PROFESSIONAL DEVELOPMENT
The school counseling team will participate in the following professional development:

_____

_____

PROFESSIONAL COLLABORATION
The school counseling department will meet weekly/monthly:

☐ As a counseling department team ☐ With administration

☐ With the school staff (faculty) ☐ With subject area departments

☐ With the advisory council

OFFICE ORGANIZATION
Responsibilities for the support services provided the counseling team will be divided among the support services staff :

The school counseling assistant will: _____ The registrar will: _____

The clerk will: _____ The receptionist will: _____

Volunteers will: _____ Others will: _____

How will the agreement be monitored during the school year? _____

_____   _____

Counselor signature & date   Principal signature & date

6. Advisory Council

Attach a list of all your school counseling program advisory council members, along with their stakeholder positions (ie, are they parents, faculty, community members, etc.). Also attach the agendas and minutes from two advisory council meetings.

Advisory Council Scoring Rubric			
4	**3**	**2**	**1**
A strong advisory council exists with representatives from core stakeholder groups. Agendas and minutes from two meetings that reflect productive work related to the school counseling program mission and goals are included.	An advisory council exists with representatives from core stakeholder groups. Agendas and minutes from two meetings that reflect the work of the council are included.	An advisory council with representatives from some core stakeholder groups exists. Agendas and minutes from two meetings are included.	No advisory council exists.

7. Calendar

Attach a copy of your school counseling master calendar for the academic year. The calendar should include all school counseling activities and events for the year for the entire counseling program. Also include one detailed weekly calendar for each counselor in the school.

Calendar Scoring Rubric			
4	**3**	**2**	**1**
Comprehensive master and weekly calendars for each counselor in the school reflect prioritized ASCA National Standards and delivery system priorities as outlined in the management agreements and school counseling program goals. .	Master and weekly calendars reflect prioritized ASCA National Standards and delivery system priorities and school counseling program goals.	Weak master and weekly calendars reflecting some delivery system priorities are included.	No master//weekly calendar is included.

C. DELIVERY

8. Classroom Curriculum

Attach the lesson plans from one classroom guidance unit conducted by a counselor in the school during the year you have designated. You may use the following template or submit your own.

Classroom Curriculum Scoring Rubric

4	**3**	**2**	**1**
A strong classroom guidance unit directly tied to the ASCA National Standards and linked to ASCA or school competencies and school counseling program goals is included. The unit is comprehensive enough to enable students to master the appropriate standards and competencies/indicators. Appropriate and relevant evaluation data for the lesson are included.	Classroom guidance unit is complete, tied to the ASCA National Standards and linked to ASCA or school competencies/indicators. Appropriate evaluation data for the lesson is included.	A weak or partial classroom guidance unit not tied to the ASCA National Standards and ASCA or school competencies/indicators. Minimal evaluation data for the lesson may be included.	No classroom guidance unit included.

Template: Classroom Guidance

Counselor Name _____ *School* _____

Title of Lesson _____ *Quarter* _____

Grade Level _____ *Time Required* _____

ASCA National Standard(s):

Competency(ies) Addressed

Material/Resources:

Activity

Evaluation (should include either process, perception and/or results data and how evaluation was conducted)
(Attach additional documentation as needed.)

9. Small-Group Curriculum

Attach the session plans for a small-group unit (either appraisal, advisement or responsive services) that was conducted by a counselor at your school during the designated school year. The unit must contain at least two sessions. You may use the template on the next page or submit one of your own.

Small-Group Curriculum Scoring Rubric

4	3	2	1
An exemplary small group unit of at least two sessions is included. The unit is directly tied to the ASCA National Standards or school competencies/indicators and school counseling program goals. The unit is comprehensive enough to enable students to master the appropriate standards and competencies/indicators. Appropriate and relevant evaluation data for the unit are included.	A satisfactory small group unit of at least four sessions directly tied to the ASCA National Standards and linked to ASCA or school competencies/indicators and school counseling program goals is included. Appropriate and relevant evaluation data for the unit are included.	A weak or incomplete small group unit that may be tied to the ASCA National Standards and linked to ASCA or school competencies/indicators is included. Some evaluation data for the unit may be included.	No small group unit included.

Template: Small-Group Guidance

Counselor Name _____ School _____

Title of Lesson _____ Quarter _____

Grade Level _____ Time Required _____

ASCA National Standard(s):

Competency(ies) Addressed

Material/Resources:

Activity

Evaluation (should include either process, perception and/or results data and how evaluation was conducted)
(Attach additional documentation as needed.)

D. ACCOUNTABILITY

10. Guidance Curriculum Results Report

Attach a guidance curriculum results report for at least four different guidance curriculum activities. You may use the following template or your own materials.

Guidance Curriculum Results Report Scoring Rubric

4	**3**	**2**	**1**
An exemplary guidance curriculum results report that reflects the ASCA National Standards, school competencies/ indicators and school counseling program goals. The report includes guidance lesson contents; number of lessons delivered and how they are delivered; start and end dates; and perception, process and results data. Additional data, relevant examples and documentation are included.	An adequate guidance curriculum results report that reflects the ASCA National Standards, school competencies/ indicators and school counseling program goals. The report includes guidance lesson contents; number of lessons delivered and how they are delivered; start and end dates; and perception, process and results data. Additional data, relevant examples and documentation are included.	A weak guidance curriculum report that does not necessarily reflect the ASCA National Standards and school competencies/indicators. Supplemental information is lacking.	An incomplete or no guidance curriculum results report is included.

AMERICAN
SCHOOL
COUNSELOR
ASSOCIATION

XYZ SCHOOL DISTRICT

Guidance Curriculum Results Report

Year _____

Grade Level	Guidance Lesson Content	Standards, Competencies, Indicators Addressed	Number of Guidance Lessons Delivered in What Class or Subject	Start Date End Date	PROCESS DATA (Number of students affected)	PERCEPTION DATA (Pre and post test competency attainment or student data)*	RESULTS DATA (How did the student change as a result of the lesson?)*	Implications (What do the data tell you?)

*Attach data, examples and documentation

_____   _____   _____
Principal's Signature   Date   Prepared by

11. Closing the Gap Results Report

Attach results from a closing-the-gap activity. Include documentation/data on how this gap was identified and why it was important to address at this time.

Closing the Gap Results Report Scoring Rubric			
4	**3**	**2**	**1**
An exemplary closing the gap results report addressing a need in the school that reflects the ASCA National Standards and school competencies/indicators. The report includes: the target group, the type of services delivered and in what manner, the start and end date, process data, perception data, results data and implications from the data. Supplemental/supporting documentation is also included.	A closing the gap results report addressing a need in the school. The report includes at least six of the following components: the target group, the curriculum and material used, the type of services delivered and in what manner, the start and end date, process data, perception data, results data, implications from the data. Supporting documentation is also included.	A weak closing the gap results report that minimally addresses a need in the school. Supplemental documentation is lacking.	An incomplete closing the gap results report. No supplemental documentation is included.

AMERICAN
SCHOOL
COUNSELOR
ASSOCIATION

XYZ SCHOOL DISTRICT

XYZ Closing the Gap Results Report

Year _____

Counselor	Target Group	Standards, Competencies, Indicators Addressed	Type of Service Delivered in What Manner?	Start Date End Date	PROCESS DATA (Number of students affected)	PERCEPTION DATA (Pre and post test competency attainment or student data)*	RESULTS DATA (How did the student change as a result of the lesson?)*	Implications (What do the data tell you?)
Berry	8th Grade: 64 students in danger of being retained at the end of trimester one	Standard A Competency A2 & A3 Indicator A:A2.1 & A:A3.1	Academic Counseling Groups Peer Mentoring	Sept 2002 June 2003	64	*Immediate* 99% correct on post-test knowledge of promotion information.	*Intermediate* 46 (72%) demonstrated improvement in GPA from Trimester 1 to Trimester 3. *Long term* 85% of at risk students showed improvement in GPA from Trimester 1 to Trimester 2.	Excellent academic improvement. Re-evaluate the curriculum used. Participants in the academic support groups may need further encouragement from other resources such as adult mentors.

Principal's Signature _____   Date _____

Prepared by _____

*Attach data, examples and documentation

12. Program Evaluation Reflection

How does your comprehensive school counseling program use advocacy, leadership, systemic change and collaboration to make a difference for students in the following areas?

(Responses should be at least 500 words and no more than 1,500.)

Program Evaluation Reflection Scoring Rubric			
4	**3**	**2**	**1**
A strong, thorough and organized response. Shows through the use of specific details and examples how the school counseling program uses advocacy, leadership, systemic change and collaboration to benefit students.	A thorough and organized response. Shows through the use of details and examples how the school counseling program uses advocacy, leadership, systemic change and collaboration to benefit students.	A weak response. Minimally shows how the school counseling program uses advocacy, leadership, systemic change and collaboration to benefit students.	An inadequate response. Does not show how the school counseling program uses advocacy, leadership, systemic change and collaboration to benefit students.